Bizarre, Baffling and Bonkers Stories
from *The Big Issue*

EDITED BY PAUL SUSSMAN

Fourth Estate • London

First published in Great Britain in 1996 by
Fourth Estate Limited
6 Salem Road
London W2 4BU

A catalogue record for this book is available from the British Library.

ISBN 1–85702–496–6

All royalties from this book go to the Big Issue Foundation.

Typeset by York House Typographic Limited, London
Printed in Great Britain by The Bath Press, Bath

CONTENTS

FOREWORD

Since its inception, *The Big Issue* has struggled to produce a magazine that has real value. From the outset, we did not simply want to rely on people's generous commitment to the homeless. The magazine had to stand on its own two feet. It had to be a good read.

Why?

If *The Big Issue* was bought only as a kind of handout, it would be a pity purchase. Homeless people would therefore be patronised in the most debilitating way. Relying on other people's hands is not good for the soul.

We wanted a wide readership magazine where the public would buy the paper because they wanted to read it. This would give an income to our vendors and at the same time be something the public appreciated. The more papers bought, the more we would be helping homeless people.

Hence, our encouragement of Mr Paul Sussman, graduate of the university of Oxford (or is it Cambridge?), to grace our pages with his wayward observations. Mr Sussman's column has proved one of the most successful features of *The Big Issue*.

Over the years, Sus, as we like to call him, has lightened our pages and won us many readers. This book is the result of his 'interesting' fertility. I do hope you buy it and enjoy it. Humour can be just as useful in helping the homeless to help themselves as more serious tracts.

John Bird

INTRODUCTION

What do you seek, gentle reader, in a genuine, boffo, bizarre tale? A *frisson* of perplexity? The sudden turn around of your teased-out expectations? Something like the end of Maupassant's famous story of seduction when the longed-for courtesan, at last in bed, leans out to switch off the light, twenty feet away? Oooheerr, missus.

Or is it just the thought, 'Coo, what a lot of weirdos there are out there'?

Here you will find the toilet-escaping butter-balled dwarf, the Love Bison betrayed, the tractor-trapped sisters, the false exploding egg. Each of these gobbets stops us in our tracks just a wee while. We ponder on the implications of these snatches – the passions, the hopes and expectations revealed, the aspirations dashed, the indignities suffered – and, I am sorry to say, allow ourselves an extended 'tee hee'.

Let's face it, as long as life contains the World's Smelliest Footwear Competition, those of us out of range are allowed to wag our heads and walk on by, sniggering.

Life's a gas and all the people in it merely molecules bumping into each other. Within these pages, those of us who are driven to distraction by the frustrations of everyday nerds will find consolation and succour. There are no prescriptions, there is nothing that can be done. These parables give us no *vade mecum*, no plan, no guidance to the road ahead – except, perhaps, to keep a look-out for what we might step in.

They merely confirm what so many of us have somehow known all along, that there is no cure for the human condition.

Let us hope we none of us get into deep water off Ravenna and solicit the help of local lifeguard Lorenzo Trippi. Lorenzo, son of the woman ox-wrestling champion of Padua, took his duties too seriously and, sadly, bumped off those he ought to have been rescuing with his over-zealous lifebelt throwing. Alas. But had we been unlucky enough to suffer this appalling fate, we could at least now take consolation in the fact that we will provide amusement for generations to come.

Deep in these tales of extreme quirk, I fear I began to meditate on what commentators have frequently called my own sad existence. How unlike my own staid and conservative self all these colourful and wilfully wacky characters are! Yes, I live rather quietly. Reading this excellent collection, I thank my lucky stars that I do.

Enjoy.

Griff Rhys Jones

Griff Rhys Jones

Stuck

One of the most frustrating things about being stuck, apart from the fact that it often chafes your skin, is that nine times out of 10 people don't realise you're stuck, and therefore don't come to your aid. Few cases demonstrate this truism more dramatically than that of Mr Gunther Burpus of Bremen, Germany, who remained wedged in his front door cat-flap for two days because passers-by thought he was a piece of installation art. Mr Burpus, 41, was using the flap because he had mislaid his door keys, unfortunately getting stuck halfway through and finding himself quite incapable of going either forwards or back. At this point he was spotted by a group of passing student pranksters who, despite his vehement protests, removed his trousers and pants, painted his bottom bright blue, jammed a daffodil between his buttocks and erected a sign on his front lawn saying, 'Germany Resurgent, an Essay in Street Art. Please give generously.' Passers-by assumed that Mr Burpus's protestations and screams were part of the act, and it was only when an old woman complained to the police that he was finally freed. 'I kept calling for help,' he explained, 'but people just said, "Very good! Very clever!" and threw coins at me.'

Eastbourne, it seems, is fast becoming the stuck capital of the northern hemisphere, especially where male genitalia are involved. Two particular cases illustrate the point. First up is Mr Albert Popplethwaite, 68, who required surgery and extensive applications of Vaseline to remove a padlock clamped around his scrotum after a home experiment went horribly wrong. 'I just wanted to see what it was like to be tortured by the Russians,' he explained reasonably. Equally embarrassing, although possibly more excruciating, were the experiences of pensioner Ron Tupper, who had to be cut free by firemen after his testicles got trapped between the slats of his sun lounger. Mr Tupper, 71, was lying naked on the plastic recliner reading a Jilly Cooper novel when disaster struck. It seems that he tried to stand up but was unable to do so because his testicles had mysteriously swollen to over twice the width of the gap through which they had dropped. He somehow shuffled his way indoors – the lounger banging between his legs like a swing-bridge – and phoned the fire brigade, who endeavoured to slip him free with a variety of lubricants, including axle-grease, baby oil and margarine. When this failed, they demolished the chair with an oxy-acetylene torch. 'Poor old guy,' said one rescuer. 'He looked like he was sitting on a pair of coconuts.'

Narrow, confined, soot-filled and vertical, chimneys should always be treated with the utmost respect and caution. Sadly Swede Sven Petersson failed to do so, spending, as a result, an uncomfortable five hours stuck down one dressed as a giant prawn. Mr Petersson, 22, of Stockholm was at a fancy-dress party in an exclusive hotel when disaster struck. Having drunk heavily all night – 'At least three bottles of champagne and 16 of lager,' he later claimed proudly – the sozzled shellfish had made his way up to the hotel roof for a breath of fresh air. Overcome by nausea, however, he had collapsed beside a chimney stack and proceeded to throw up down it. 'God knows how it happened,' he said, 'but I just lost my footing and ended up falling down the flue head-first. I tumbled about 40 feet and then got wedged in a narrow part of the pipe. I kept calling for help and eventually someone heard me and shouted, "Who are you?" I said, "The Icelandic Prawn with nylon feelers", which is when they called the police.' A complex rescue operation was mounted, with firemen finally having to drill through a bedroom wall to recover the cramped crustacean. 'It's a shame we didn't bring some lettuce and Thousand Island dressing,' quipped one rescuer.

All firemen deal with at least one stuck person during the course of their careers, although it is unlikely to be anyone quite as stuck as Mr Albert Timmins, 61, of Chicago. Rescuers were alerted to Mr Timmins's predicament by a phone call from a hysterical woman screaming, 'Dear God, it's collapsed! He's trapped! Trapped!' They immediately swung into action, leaping on to their fire engines, and with lights flashing and sirens blaring charged to the rescue. 'We thought it was probably some sort of structural collapse,' explained fire chief Andy Crenshaw. 'These things have to be approached with extreme caution, so we evacuated neighbours and went in very carefully, wearing oxygen masks in case there were escaped gases.' To their surprise, however, the firemen discovered not escaped gases but a red-faced Mr Timmins 'trussed-up like a groundhog'. 'He was shackled to a giant mousetrap with his penis on a complex pulley system,' recalled chief Crenshaw. 'It looked absolutely agonising.' It took rescuers two hours of 'heavy cutting' and a lot of baby oil to free Mr Timmins, who later claimed he was conducting 'a perfectly valid experiment into the effects of high-velocity space travel'.

At one point or another most of us have had nightmares about being stuck in a lift. For New Zealander Brenda Shine, however, the nightmare became reality when she spent three days trapped in the elevator of a multistorey car park after it got stuck between floors. Mrs Shine, 69, of Auckland was ascending to her car after doing the weekly shopping when the lift suddenly juddered to a halt. 'I screamed for help,' she explained, 'but the only person who heard me laughed and said, "Blow it out your arse, you old bat!" which I found very demoralising.' She was too short to reach the trapdoor in the lift ceiling, whilst attempts to draw attention to her predicament by banging a cucumber against the metal walls had to be abandoned after the vegetable disintegrated in her hands. After 72 hours, during which time she tap-danced almost continually in order to keep warm, the lift suddenly started working again of its own volition. Even then, however, Mrs Shine's misfortunes weren't over, as she had to pay a substantial fine to get her car out of the car park because her ticket had expired. 'I tried to explain,' she said, 'but the attendant said I stank and ought to be ashamed of myself.'

They're such obviously small and confined spaces, it's amazing more people don't get stuck in telephone boxes. One who did, in a most dramatic manner, was travelling sales executive Pedro Samosa, who spent two days trapped in a call box in a remote and mountainous region of northern Spain. Mr Samosa, 36, of Madrid was returning home after an important sales conference when he decided to stop at the call box and telephone his wife, duly parking his car on a slight slope some 10 feet away from the kiosk and ensconcing himself therein. On discovering it was out of order, however, he turned to leave the cabin, only to see his car rolling down the slope towards him. 'The handbrake must have slipped,' he said. 'I tried to get out but I wasn't quick enough and it crashed right into the door, wedging me inside.' Despite frantic efforts, Mr Samosa was unable to force the door open. Neither was he able to break through the thick Perspex sides of the cabin, whilst his attempts to attract passing motorists were met with 'waves and friendly hoots'. He was eventually saved, 48 hours later, by a lemon farmer who noticed him slumped in a heap on the phone-box floor. 'He'll have to pay to have the cabin cleaned,' said a local policeman. 'It was disgustingly smelly.'

Although the Dordogne is one of the most hospitable regions of France, it proved an unfortunate holiday choice for elderly spinsters Lucille and Claudette Mammouth, who spent almost their entire summer vacation trapped inside an unheated cottage as a result of a badly parked tractor. Trouble started when a local farmer, believing the cottage to be empty, left his tractor and attached manure spreader wedged against the front door. Unbeknown to him, however, the Mammouth sisters, 79 and 82 respectively, were inside, knitting and enjoying the first day of their holiday. 'We heard a noise so we went to investigate,' explained Claudette. 'But when we opened the door the tractor was in the way and we couldn't get out. We hit it with a rolling pin, and Lucille tried to crawl underneath, but her glasses steamed up and she had to come back.' After desperately calling for help, the sisters tried to crawl out of a window, 'but our bottoms were too big', whilst an attempt to clamber up the chimney had to be abandoned when Claudette was bitten by a nesting squirrel. Eventually they made a cup of tea, resumed their knitting and waited patiently for their unwitting captor to return, which he did a week later. 'You'd think we'd be scared,' declared Lucille, 'but the time just flew by. Before we knew it we'd done six jumpers, a scarf and eight pairs of mittens.'

There are 101 exciting things you can do with concrete, but going to sleep in it isn't one of them. Such was certainly the experience of the unfortunately named Grant Shittit, who spent three days trapped in a hole full of the stuff after inadvertently lying down on it for a quick snooze. Following 'a real humdinger of a booze-up', an inebriated Mr Shittit, 41, of Timaru, New Zealand, was returning on foot to his remote farmstead home when he felt the need to prostrate himself by the roadside 'and recover my strength'. Locating what he took to be a bed 'of lovely soft moss', he duly removed his shoes, stretched himself out and fell into a deep slumber, waking up the next morning to find himself stuck fast in a trench full of cement. 'Only my head was free,' he later explained. 'Everything else from my neck down was wedged solid. It was particularly uncomfortable because I'd been sick on myself in the night and there was a little puddle of it right under my nose.' Despite repeated cries for help, he wasn't spotted for nearly 72 hours, and only then by a motorist who stopped because she thought he was an injured hedgehog. He was freed by firemen using pneumatic drills and made a full recovery. 'I was completely and utterly stoned,' he quipped.

We've all suffered the inconvenience of being locked out of our house or flat at some point in our lives. Few of us, however, can have been as inconvenienced as Norwegian house-sitter Sven Hengel, who spent two days standing nude in a wheelie bin after his front door inadvertently slammed shut behind him. Unemployed Mr Hengel, 34, was house-sitting for a friend in Oslo when disaster struck. 'I was in the shower when I thought I heard the doorbell ring,' explained Mr Hengel, 'so I rushed downstairs and said through the letter box, "Who is there?" When no one answered, I opened the door and stepped outside, and a gust of wind just blew it shut.' Trapped on the front lawn, naked and soapy, in sub-zero temperatures, Mr Hengel initially hid himself in a large bush and called for help, but no one heard him save for two youths on mountain bicycles who shouted 'Willy-sucker!' before cycling away at top speed. He then attempted to climb up the outside of the house towards an open bedroom window, but lost his footing and tumbled 15 feet into a snow drift, breaking two ribs. He eventually took refuge in a wheelie bin on the front doorstep, insulating himself with leaves and a goodly supply of malodorous household refuse, and patiently waited for his householder friend to return, which he duly did two days later. 'I could have gone to find a phone,' said Mr Hengel, recovering in hospital from hypothermia, 'but I'd promised I'd watch the house and friendship is about keeping your promises.'

Rare indeed is the person who hasn't, at one point or another, wanted to do something awful to their bank manager. For most of us, however, the something awful remains a pleasing if unfulfilled fantasy. Not so Frenchwoman Jacqueline Leclair, who, after being refused a £200 loan, exacted a terrible revenge by supergluing herself to her shocked local branch manager. Ms Leclair, 30, had gone into the bank hoping to secure a loan in order to buy a new dress. When she was informed by the manager that such a thing 'would be quite out of the question', however, she went berserk, calling him a 'flabby, four-eyed faggot' before being hustled out of the door by two cashiers. Two hours later she was back, however, and, stripping to her underwear in front of horrified customers, smeared herself head to toe in superglue. When the manager remonstrated, she screamed, 'Together for ever till I get my money!' and threw herself at him, bonding immediately with his double-breasted salmon-pink Armani suit. They remained thus for two hours until doctors were able to separate them with solvents. 'It was a sticky situation,' quipped Ms Leclair's victim, demonstrating that bank managers are, after all, extraordinarily witty people.

In the annals of police bravery few can occupy a more exalted place than 23-stone American police officer Levett Sponge, whose attempts to foil a bank raid were themselves foiled when he got wedged in a revolving door. Officer Sponge, 30, of Seattle was out on foot patrol when he spotted two men entering a bank wearing masks and armed with shotguns. Without a thought for his own safety, he immediately drew his gun and launched himself at the bank's revolving doorway, which, on account of his substantial girth, got stuck mid-rotation, pinning his gun arm into his face and leaving him to watch helplessly as the laughing thieves calmly completed their robbery. 'He was all squashed up against the glass, like a huge strawberry in a liquidiser,' recalled one terrified customer. 'He shouted, "Good will triumph in the end," but the thieves just said, "Unless it's fat and stuck in a revolving door," which made him go very quiet.' The robbers' amusement was cut short, however, when they discovered that the revolving door was the only exit from the building and, after frantic efforts to de-rotate officer Sponge, they were forced to surrender. 'Sponge is a true American hero,' gushed one senior policeman.

TOWN WIN
REF SHOOTS PLAYER
LOCAL NEWS
WOMAN POISONS HUSBAND!
TURN TO PAGE TWO
PSSST
FLY SPRAY

Love

Some people will go to extreme lengths in the quest for romantic fulfilment. Witness Herman Marble, of Kite, Dakota, who began acting very strangely when he fell for his secretary, Ethel Pripp. Initially Mr Marble began leaving perfumed notes on Miss Pripp's desk, announcing that 'Puppy's got a bone, woofy-woo!' Surprisingly, however, this failed to have the desired effect, so he took to posting himself to her house inside a large gift-wrapped cardboard box marked: 'Handle with care – insemination equipment inside.' When this didn't work either, he decided drastic measures were needed, parachuting into her garden dressed as a giant lobster with a bunch of roses clutched in his claw. It would be nice to report that, after so much effort, the pair are now lovers, but sadly it was not to be, for as Mr Marble descended from the sky, Miss Pripp's grandfather mistook him for an alien and shot him in the tail. He is now planning an 'all-out love attack' on one of the nurses who tended him. 'She's never seen such a massive shellfish!' he declared proudly.

Having a proposal of marriage rejected is a deeply depressing occurrence, although few people react quite as badly as Frenchman Jean Aliers did when his girlfriend rebuffed him 20,000 feet up in the air. Mr Aliers, 34, of Rouen had met Margaret Lefebre at a local skydiving club. The free-falling couple had fallen madly in love and, after an intense two-year romance, Mr Aliers decided the time had come to cement their relationship by getting married. He had duly proposed in the middle of a jump, pulling a bunch of squashed flowers from his jump-suit pocket and presenting Ms Lefebre with a diamond ring. To his horror, however, she screamed in his ear, 'I can't! I'm screwing your father!' to which, without further ado, he screamed back, 'I'm strawberry jam, you bitch, and it's your fault!' before unharnessing his parachute and tumbling earthwards to his death. His girlfriend was devastated, not least because 'It was just a little joke and I wanted to marry him more than anyone else in the world.'

Stag parties can be notoriously bad news for the man about to be married, although few can have ended quite as disastrously as that of Swiss groom-to-be Artur Schasser. Mr Schasser had gone away with friends to the Olympic skiing resort of Lillehammer. Here the group had indulged in a herculean drinking session before gathering their equipment and heading up into the hills for a spot of night-time downhill. At precisely the same moment, totally independent of the male party and unbeknown to them, Mr Schasser's fiancée, Clara Glumbrucht, was herself skiing further down the same slope with her father, Helmut, and a group of old schoolfriends. For a while it looked as if everything would be OK and the two groups wouldn't meet – until, that is, Artur's friends decided to strip him naked, tie him in a kneeling position on a large red Lilo and dispatch him bottom-first down the snowy incline. 'I was looking between my legs,' said Artur, 'and suddenly saw people below me. I shouted, "Beware!" but the wind was so strong in my face that poor Mr Glumbrucht didn't hear me.' The nude groom careered into his prospective father-in-law bottom first, killing him instantly and ricocheting into another woman, whose shoulder was broken. The engagement has since been called off.

Urgent warning to all bridegrooms-to-be: always tell your fiancée everything about yourself before you get married, otherwise you might end up having the sort of nightmare honeymoon experienced by Spanish groom Fritz Neumair. Mr Neumair's wedding day had, in his own words, been 'the most wonderful day of my life'. The church service and buffet reception had all gone off without a hitch, the bride and groom's families had mingled sociably, the speeches had been funny and 'everything had been as perfect as perfect could be'. Mr Neumair and his bride, Maria, had booked for their honeymoon into an exclusive lakeside hotel, and it was here, as they tucked up for their first night as a married couple, that things started to go disastrously wrong. It appears that during their whirlwind romance Mr Neumair had neglected to inform his fiancée that he wore a wig. She was thus surprised when, during a strenuous bout of post-nuptial lovemaking, her husband's scalp dropped off and stuck to her chest. 'She went totally hysterical and said she'd divorce me unless I ate the toupee,' explained the hairless husband. 'I asked if I could put some ketchup on it, but she said no and called me "slap-head", which I found rather offensive.' Desperate to save his day-old marriage, Mr Neumair grudgingly complied with his wife's gastronomic wishes, only to be told, on completion of his hirsute repast, that she was divorcing him anyway. 'I married him for his hair,' she explained. 'It looked like silk spun in heaven.'

Seeing the one you love marry another person is bad enough, but when you end up being pelted with pretzels and smoked salmon sandwiches by the wedding party, you know Destiny's really got it in for you. Such was the cruel fate of failed lover Simon Zadich, 27, of Warsaw, whose last-ditch attempt to win back childhood sweetheart Anna ended with him ignominiously buried beneath a mound of hors-d'oeuvres. Mr Zadich had been devastated when he heard of Anna's forthcoming marriage to a tractor mechanic. When a series of 293 pleading letters failed to dissuade her from the union, however, he decided more direct action was needed, bursting into the wedding reception, firing a gun in the air and screaming, 'Oh, she was pretty as a peach! Let her be mine again.'

A horrified silence was broken when the bride's mother threw a large pickled gherkin at the tormented lover, hitting him on the forehead. Other guests joined in, chanting, "Lonely!" and pelting the weeping Lothario with an assortment of crustless sandwiches and condiments until he eventually collapsed under a welter of pastries and stewed fruit. 'I gave her my heart,' said Zadich, 'but she threw it back in a mushroom vol-au-vent.'

Lovemaking should be one of the most beautiful, fulfilling and exceedingly sweaty aspects of any relationship. Unfortunately, it didn't work out like that for the Birpitzes of Düsseldorf when, during a particularly frenzied bout of coital interaction, Mrs Birpitz accidentally bit off her husband's nose. Arnie and Nathalie Birpitz, 47 and 43 respectively, enjoyed a peculiarly idiosyncratic sex life, being, on this particular occasion, dressed as World War Two stormtroopers, complete with tin helmets and hand grenades. 'We were doing what all lovers do,' explained a bandaged Mr Birpitz, 'when she started sucking my nose, really hard, like a vacuum cleaner. I said, "Please don't do that, Nathalie, it's unhygienic!" but she just moaned louder and louder and then bit it off.' Mr Birpitz – still sporting full World War Two regalia – was rushed to hospital, where the tip of his nose was successfully sewn back on. 'We've told neighbours I had a gardening accident,' he said later. 'The truth would be too much for them to take.'

Greater love hath no man for his wife than to wait for her in a supermarket car park. Except, that is, to wait for her for seven days in a supermarket car park, which is what 78-year-old Alberto Sciaffa did whilst his wife busied herself with the weekly shopping. Mr Sciaffa of Turin had dropped his wife off at the supermarket entrance before driving into a nearby car park to await her return. Unfortunately, Mrs Sciaffa, who is apparently 'forgetful at the best of times, and a positive amnesiac when she's doing the shopping', completely forgot that he was there, returning home on a bus and then reporting her husband missing when he failed to come home for his tea. Mr Sciaffa, meanwhile, sat patiently in his Fiat Uno, humming and playing noughts and crosses with himself. 'I thought she was taking a long time,' he explained, 'but she often lingers around the pesto sauces, and I didn't want to leave the car in case she came back and got worried.' Instead he lived off boiled sweets and radiator water, relieving himself in the car boot because 'it would be dirty to go on the pavement'. He was eventually discovered a week later by supermarket staff, who had received complaints about 'a filthy old man in the car park'. 'It was a long wait, but it was worth it,' said Mr Sciaffa. 'I love my wife very much.'

Some men want nothing more than a wife who will clean the house, do the shopping and make dinner. As Victor Opal of Bedfordshire discovered, however, you can have too much of a good thing. Every day for 40 years Mr Opal, 68, was forced to listen to his wife 'wittering on about disinfectants and toilet ducks and lavender wax polish – on and on and on, like a torture. She lived for her housekeeping. The woman was totally obsessed.' The hounded husband would often be woken in the middle of the night so that his wife could, on a whim, hoover under the bed, whilst he was once forced to stay in a hotel for three days so that she could 'give the bathroom a really proper clean'. Things came to a head during a Sunday afternoon drive in the country when Mrs Opal, who was at the wheel, began complaining about the price of lemons. 'I don't know what sparked it off,' said Mr Opal, 'but I just flipped. I thought, "Sod bloody lemons!", opened the door and threw myself out, even though we were doing

50 mph.' Despite suffering a fractured skull and multiple lacerations, Mr Opal feels his protest was worth it. 'She hasn't touched the Mr Sheen for over a week,' he said. 'It feels like we're on honeymoon again.'

Being a henpecked husband is one thing, being a hen-savaged husband quite another, as discovered by Sicilian spouse Lorenzo Berti, who underwent eight years of vicious ill-treatment at the hands of 19-stone wife Magdalena. Things started to go wrong for Mr Berti in 1988 when, some four days after their marriage, his wife informed him he hadn't done the washing up properly and would therefore have to be flogged. 'I'd left some egg on a plate,' he explained, 'so she tanned my bottom with a garden trowel.' For a while it looked as if this might be an unfortunate one-off, but when she broke his nose for failing to spray the toilet after using it Mr Berti realised his married life was not destined to be a happy one. Before long Mrs Berti had decreed that her partner must sleep handcuffed in a cupboard, wear only a pinny and espadrilles in her presence and spend all day doing menial household chores. 'It was a living nightmare,' he recalled. 'I once forgot to polish the tomatoes before she chopped them for dinner. She practically beat me to death with a rolling pin.' The hounded husband was eventually liberated from his misery by police after a tip-off from neighbours, and now lives with his mother in Palermo. 'She was a big woman, but I still believe she loved me in her own way,' he claims.

Most marital tiffs are over petty things such as washing up and who sleeps on which side of the bed. An altogether more dramatic row flared up between a couple in China, however, after a man spent three years copying the entire works of Confucius on to the back of a postage stamp only to see his masterpiece stuck on a postcard and mailed to his mother-in-law. Mr Zhang Keige of Xuzhou had, by his own admission, become 'obsessed' with the Confucius project, working every day for 18 hours until it was finished. 'When it was complete I cried tears of joy, offered up a silent prayer and then went to the toilet for relief,' he explained. 'It was a good relief, and a long one, but when I returned to my study I found that the stamp had gone.' A frantic search of the house proved fruitless, and only when his wife informed him she'd just sent a card to her mother to tell her of the completion of her spouse's work did the horrible truth dawn. 'I screamed, "Are you stupid?"' said a devastated Mr Keige, 'but she said, "No, I am a woman," which I couldn't very well deny.' He now intends to copy the full works of Chairman Mao on to a matchstick.

Few things can be more detrimental to a marriage than suspicion, as discovered by Australian Lucas Eggspot after his wife found a lipstick-smeared toothbrush in the back of his car. Mr and Mrs Eggspot, 55 and 53 respectively, had been married for over 30 years, with barely a cross word spoken between them in all that time. Everything changed, however, with the discovery of the toothbrush. Convinced it was evidence of an illicit sexual liaison 'with someone younger and less saggy' than herself, Mrs Eggspot embarked on a campaign of retribution against her wayward husband. It started with relatively innocuous measures such as lacing his dinner with powdered laxative, setting light to his carpet slippers – whilst he was still in them – and destroying his car with a pickaxe. Things soon escalated, however, with a frenzied Mrs Eggspot knocking her spouse unconscious with a saucepan and imprisoning him in an upstairs cupboard from which she refused to release him until he confessed 'to each and every poke'. Only when it transpired that the toothbrush actually belonged to her mother-in-law did Mrs Eggspot relent, releasing her bruised husband and baking him a cake by way of apology. 'Actually, I was rather flattered,' he later admitted. 'It shows how much she loves me.'

In an age of disastrous marriages, one of the most disastrous of all has to be that of Kurt and Felicia Carney of Florida. Mr and Mrs Carney, 36 and 33 respectively, had met whilst on holiday in Atlantic City and were married soon afterwards. From the first, however, it was a stormy relationship. 'She was a big blonde girl,' explained Mr Carney, 'and a bit of a law unto herself. She refused to have sex with me and got very upset if I tried to look at her undressing. She also liked baseball and drank a lot of Budweiser.' Initially he was prepared to overlook these idiosyncrasies, but as their marriage progressed so things gradually deteriorated, with his spouse regularly beating him at arm-wrestling and showing an increasingly unladylike fascination for drag-car racing and pornographic videos. Things came to a head one drunken evening when Mr Carney refused to go to the shops to purchase a six-pack of beer for his beloved, whereupon she punched him in the face and put him in a headlock. 'I said, "That's not how a woman should act!" ' recalled the humiliated husband, 'and the next thing I knew she was shaking a blonde wig in my face and shouting, "That's because I'm not a woman, you jerk-off!" ' Felicia, it appeared, was actually Felix, an unemployed car mechanic who had dressed up as a woman 'for a laugh' but had discovered, once married, that he 'rather enjoyed being loved and pampered', and had therefore maintained the charade for two years. 'It was a shame, because my parents adored her,' said a disappointed Mr Carney.

There are a host of reasons why marriages break up, although failure to grunt during lovemaking is not usually one of them. Such, however, was the cause cited by an Israeli woman who divorced her husband of four years for failing to 'groan, snort, squeal or moan' during coitus. Ruth and Yari Cohen, 36 and 35 respectively, of Jerusalem were, outwardly at least, the perfect couple. They had two children, good jobs, a nice house – all the trappings of a happy marriage. This harmonious exterior, however, concealed a terrible secret: Mr Cohen was a silent lovemaker. 'There was nothing wrong with his size or technique,' explained his wife, 'but he never made any noise. You could hear a pin drop. I used to slap him and say, "Come on, groan!" and he'd go, "Oh! Oh! Oh!" and that was it. You'd have got more expression out of an insulation brick.' Despite various schemes to elicit sound from her spouse, including engaging him in heated political debate during sex and jabbing a knitting needle into his buttock at the point of orgasm, Mr Cohen's lovemaking remained resolutely and steadfastly mute. The couple have now been granted a divorce, and Mrs Cohen is dating a traffic policeman. 'He screams, "Move along, please!"' she enthused. 'It's so passionate.'

Probably the most extended marriage breakdown of all time occurred in Iran, where a 105-year-old man divorced his 100-year-old wife on the grounds that he hadn't trusted her for the last 82 years. Mohammed Bahrami married childhood sweetheart Tamza in 1912. All went well for the first two years of their marriage, with the couple being, by all accounts, 'the happiest husband and wife in the world'. Around 1915, however, Mr Bahrami started to doubt his wife's fidelity after he spotted her handing a peeled onion to a male neighbour. After that he kept a close watch and his suspicions appeared to be confirmed 16 years later in 1931, when he found her singing in the bathroom. Still he gave her the benefit of the doubt, however, for, as he explained, 'I am not a jealous man and believe one must think good of all people.' Over the ensuing

65 years, however, a spate of incidents, including a badly washed spoon in 1956 and a mislaid sock in the early 1970s, persuaded the long-suffering Mr Bahrami that his wife was 'faithless as a fat marsh toad'. Things came to a head on their 84th wedding anniversary, when Mrs Bahrami refused to massage her husband's feet, whereupon he finally accused her of 'screwing around' and filed for divorce. 'Now I wish to start a new life,' he declared, 'free of suspicion.'

Forget marriage guidance counselling and quickie divorces, the thing to do if you're not getting on with your husband is to bump him off. This was just the course decided upon by German spouse Herga Fartalus, 51, who hatched a diabolical plan to kill husband Nester with a fly-spray sandwich. The repellent insect-repellent scheme was the culmination of a series of murder attempts by Mrs Fartalus, who had fallen out with her husband because he left dandruff on the pillow and wouldn't let her watch game shows on television. 'At first I tried dropping bricks on him from an upstairs window,' she explained, 'but they kept missing. Then I tried to stab him with a spoon, but he thought I was just being coy and we had to make love.' Various other bizarre schemes proved equally fruitless, and it was only when she hit upon the fly-spray plan that she felt her luck was turning. 'I read on the label that fly spray kills flies,' she recalled, 'so I thought, "And why not husbands too?" I therefore made him a sandwich and put a bit of spray on it and told him it was a delicious new spread.' After one bite, however, Mr Fartalus became suspicious and confronted his wife, who broke down in tears and told him the truth, whereupon he had her arrested. She was brought to trial, but judges gave her a suspended sentence because 'there wasn't even enough spray on the bread to kill an amoeba'.

Mind, Body and Spirit

Britain's Health Service might be in decline, but fortunately we haven't yet reached the stage where transplant patients feel obliged to bring along their own replacement organs. It's an altogether different story in Argentina, where road-sweeper Hector Paez presented his GP with a pair of perfectly fresh eyeballs and asked him to surgically insert them in place of his existing ones. Mr Paez, a chronic cataract sufferer, had stolen the 'lovely sparkly eyes' from a local hospital, concealing them in a pickle jar beneath his bed before asking his doctor to swap them for his old orbs. When the latter refused, Mr Paez went berserk, stamping on the eyes and screaming, 'If I can't have them nobody will!' He later claimed he had found them sitting on a park bench, where the owner 'must have left them while he was having a sandwich'.

Although they have some of the best beer and finest bratwurst in the world, Germany is not the place to go if you're contemplating an operation on your penis. Witness the disasters that befell Mr Friedrich Sukker, 42, of Munich, who awoke from a routine genital operation to discover what looked like 'an item of medieval nautical equipment' lurking between his legs. Mr Sukker had gone into hospital to have a special implant inserted into his penis to straighten it up. 'It was rather bent in the middle,' he explained, 'like one of those Uri Geller spoons. I wanted a straight penis, something I could measure with ease and use without embarrassment.' Due to an administrative error, however, Mr Sukker's long-awaited implant was inserted upside-down, thereby exacerbating his organ's already pronounced camber. 'I woke from the operation and there it was, lying on my leg, all bandaged up,' recalled Mr Sukker. 'I just screamed. It looked like a sextant.' Doctors have promised to redo the operation, but Mr Sukker is not satisfied. 'The nurses laughed behind my back,' he complained bitterly, 'and called me the Corkscrew.'

Americans appear to have stumbled across the ideal way of improving their physiques – eat as much as you want, but have your photographs doctored to make you appear less fat than you actually are. Across the States photographic processing firms are doing a brisk business in the distortion of holiday snaps, making even the most obese of sunbathers look like something out of *Baywatch*. Occasionally, however, things can go wrong, as discovered by 18-stone sales manager John Muttins, who sent a series of holiday slides in for doctoring, only to receive them back looking fatter than he actually was. Mr Muttins had sent off the slides as soon as he returned from holiday in Hawaii, providing strict instructions that his voluminous belly, breasts and buttocks should be airbrushed out and replaced with something 'a bit tauter and more manly'. Unfortunately, the slides were delivered to the wrong address – a student fraternity house whose inhabitants, as a joke, took them to a photographic studio and had all the salient features enhanced rather than reduced before returning them to an unsuspecting Mr Muttins. 'I had invited a load of people round to see them,' explained the portly photographer, 'including Janice, a girl I really liked. The first few were all right, but then there was one of me sunbathing and I looked pregnant. In another I had breasts down to my stomach and a backside like an over-inflated beach ball. Everyone was laughing and I just burst into tears.' The story has a happy ending, however, for Janice later complimented Mr Muttins on how much weight he'd lost since the photos were taken, and they are now going out. 'Every fat buttock has a silver lining,' he commented wryly.

For some it's just a matter of eating less and putting in the odd hour on the exercise bike. For others, however, weight loss involves some altogether more exotic behaviour. One such was 29-stone self-confessed 'gut explosion' Wallace Woob of Chicago. Mr Woob had tried a variety of slimming programmes, including an all-liquid diet, hypnosis and regular herbal enemas, but, after failing to lose a single pound, had eventually turned to an 'instant slimming remedy' advertised in his local paper. This, it transpired, was a small Chinese man who, twice weekly, smothered his patient in scented oils and viciously thrashed him on the buttocks with a wooden paddle. This had little apparent effect and, a month after starting his treatment, Mr Woob was on the point of giving up when he received a lurid pornographic magazine entitled *Baron Blubber* through the post. This comprised a selection of explicit photos of himself being oiled and beaten, accompanied by such captions as 'Mr Fatty gets it on the bottom' and 'Ripple King squeals in pain'. 'It's worked,' admitted a chastened Mr Woob. 'I haven't eaten since.'

Equally extreme, equally unwelcome and ultimately less successful was the weight-loss programme unleashed upon 19-stone Timothy Toast at an exclusive Miami health spa. Like Mr Woob, Mr Toast had dabbled with a variety of slimming methods before booking himself into the $600-a-day spa as a last resort. 'I'd tried to go it alone,' he explained, 'but the lure of McDonald's was just too strong and I realised I needed professional help.' From the first, however, the spa's regime disagreed with the gluttonous guest. On arrival he was ordered to strip naked in the front hall and do 100 press-ups. When he failed to get past five he was called 'a disgustingly obese, wobbly hippo' and dispatched to the 'Fat Detention Room' for twelve hours' solitary confinement, during which he was subjected to a continual barrage of subliminal tape recordings informing him he had 'the fattest arse in the universe'. There followed seven days of extensive food rejection therapy, including near-drowning in a soup-filled Jacuzzi and daily beatings with barbecued chicken legs. 'They'd burst into my room in the middle of the night and scream "Hungry, eh?"' recounted a shell-shocked Mr Toast. 'And I'd say, "No, no, I just need sleep," and then they'd throw cream cakes at me.' At one point things got so bad that he tried to escape over a 10-foot wall but fell off and was bitten by a guard dog. 'I've put on 24 pounds since,' said the stressed slimmer. 'I'm eating to forget.'

Few experiences are more guaranteed to end in disaster than a trip to the hairdressers'. Not only are barbers the most boring people in the world, but they invariably do totally the opposite to your head of what you actually wanted them to do. This is exactly what happened to New York fashion guru Costas Poon, who went into a salon to get highlights in his luxuriant black hair and emerged sporting a peroxide blond Afro with a green pigtail and a bald patch in the middle 'like Harpo Marx meets Kermit meets the mad monk of Assisi'. Rather than just accept his dramatic new appearance, however, Mr Poon plotted revenge, kidnapping the guilty hairdresser, shaving his entire body, painting him silver and then supergluing his buttocks to the window of his shop. 'I wanted him to know what it felt like to be a real freak,' said an embittered Mr Poon from beneath a brand-new shiny black wig. 'I wanted him to feel the pain of total fashion apocalypse.'

One of the great misconceptions about psychoanalysis is that the analyst is actually any more balanced than the person he is analysing. Such was certainly not the case in Barcelona, Spain, however, where a therapist recently shot his patient after the latter told him he looked like a porky pig. Psychoanalyst Rodrigo Conchitez, 51, had been counselling Juan Torra, 33, for almost a year when disaster struck. 'He was an extremely difficult patient,' admitted Mr

Conchitez. 'He was very paranoid and would often arrive in the office with a paper bag on his head so that people didn't recognise him, which of course they did because no one else wears paper bags on their head.' Progress was gradual if slow, however, until, during a particularly emotional session, Mr Torra suddenly informed Mr Conchitez that he looked like 'a pink snouting pig'. 'I found the allusion particularly upsetting,' recalled the uppity analyst, 'because as a child everyone had called me Piggy Conchitez, which I didn't like at all. I said, "Please don't say that, Mr Torra!" but he began to make snorting sounds, which is when I lost control.' Seizing a gun from his drawer, Mr Conchitez shot the unfortunate man in the chest. 'He whispered, "Oink, oink" and then he died,' said the psychotic psychoanalyst. 'I am clearly not as harmonious a person as I once thought.'

Usually it's a fairly harmless pastime involving a nocturnal trundle around the bedroom in your pyjamas. For some people, however, sleepwalking is a far more malevolent affliction, nowhere more so than in the case of German Marcus Werning, who awoke recently to find himself trotting stark naked through the middle of Frankfurt. A lifelong somnambulist, Mr Werning, 27, had on previous occasions boiled his goldfish and weeded the garden dressed in his wife's bra and knickers, all whilst fast asleep. The 'nude in Frankfurt' scenario was, however, by its protagonist's own admission, by far the worst sleepwalk he had ever done. 'I had gone to bed as usual,' he explained, 'but when I woke up I was skipping naked through the middle of town with my briefcase and umbrella. At first I thought I was still dreaming, but then I knew by the way people were looking that it was real. It was unbelievably humiliating.' The butt-naked businessman took refuge in a toilet, but was later arrested trying to board a bus wearing nothing but a cardboard box. He has now vowed that henceforth he will handcuff himself to the bed prior to falling asleep.

Other than enormously fat old ladies who drink too much and insist on dancing in a sexually provocative manner, the one guest none of us wants to get lumbered with at a party is the social bore. Sadly that's just what happened to Mr Satar Chupperjee, whose reaction to 'the most tedious conversation in the world' now leaves him facing life imprisonment. Mr Chupperjee, 40, of Delhi was on his way to a dinner party when he was cornered on the bus by a man of quite staggering social ineptitude. 'He was extremely sweaty, and spent the whole journey talking about Tarmac,' explained a shell-shocked Mr Chupperjee. 'How it was made, where it was made, different types of it. I've never been less interested in anything in my life.' The diatribe left its unwilling recipient feeling 'morally and sexually drained' and it was thus with horror that he discovered his tormentor was going to the same party. 'He said we were friends and must sit beside each other at dinner,' said Mr Chupperjee. 'I said, "No, no, I'll go over there," but our host thought I was just being polite and put us side by side. It was terrible. Four hours on the history of tarpaulin. Eventually I just snapped.' According to fellow guests, Mr Chupperjee was heard to scream, 'Fuck tarpaulin!' before forcing his interlocutor's head into a tureen of mulligatawny soup and throwing him from a fifth-floor balcony. 'Now he talks in my dreams,' said Mr Chupperjee. 'I am cursed.'

Although they are intended to be peaceful, coming-together sort of occasions, an opportunity for like-minded people to air their views and listen to those of others, international conferences often fail to live up to expectations. Such was certainly the case in Madrid, where a multinational seminar on 'Controlling the Temper Within' had to be abandoned after delegates got cross and attacked each other. All went well for the first two days of the conference, with talks on 'How I Stopped Killing People' and 'The Politics of Genocide' being extremely well received. Things started to go horribly wrong, however, during a yoga demonstration by Mr Sundej Panti of India. Mr Panti, 47, had just assumed a complex yet relaxing position which involved placing his arms between his legs and his legs behind his head, when a thunderous fart rent the air. Sniggers echoed around the packed hall and one audience member shouted, 'Panti's parped!' whereupon the tangled yoga expert unfolded himself and charged at his accuser, crying, 'I am not wind!' 'All hell broke loose,' explained one eyewitness. 'Panti was hitting the man and shouting, "Control is all!" and then everyone else joined in.' Seventeen delegates were later arrested. 'They touched something deep within,' said the seminar's proud organiser.

For most people a trip to church once a week is more than enough to satisfy their spiritual needs. Not so in America, where the faithful are able to top up their church visits by watching 24-hour-a-day religious television and phoning special Christian telephone hotlines. Callers to one such line in Philadelphia, however, got slightly more than they bargained for when, far from urging them to acts of charity and repentance, the Holy Spirit informed them he'd got 'a lovely tight ass and tits the size of melons'. The 'Singalonga Jesus' line had been advertised in a local paper as somewhere people could call to hear and join in with 'hymns to the glory of our Lord and master Jesus Christ'. Unfortunately, typesetters in the newspaper's production department had inadvertently transposed two digits of the advertised phone number, so that far from being greeted by an array of edifying religious music callers heard a husky female voice asking 'Oooooh, you filthy dirty sexpot, why not slip off your knickers and relax with the filthiest, dirtiest sex line ever?' going on to describe in intimate detail what she looked like and what she'd like to do to them. The paper's switchboard was jammed with horrified customers, including one old man inquiring whether he could singalonga Jesus without removing his pants, 'because my flat isn't centrally heated'.

God, it seems, can do a lot of things, but driving isn't one of them. Witness the case of motorist Alessandro Bartok, who caused a huge pile-up on a German autobahn after removing his hands from the steering wheel and 'leaving Jesus to drive us home'. Mr Bartok of Verona was on holiday with his family when the incident occurred. It appears that he had talked non-stop for almost three hours about the glory of baby Jesus and his limitless powers of understanding. Eventually, bored beyond endurance, his son had muttered 'Bollocks!' whereupon Mr Bartok screamed, 'I'll show you his power!' and removed his hands from the steering wheel, pleading all the while with Jesus to 'drive your servants home and park in front of the garage'. Unfortunately, however, the Holy Spirit was unfamiliar with power steering, for after zigzagging erratically back and forth across the motorway, he smashed into the back of a lorry, causing an 18-car pile-up. 'It was a miracle no one was killed,' declared a triumphant Mr Bartok.

Christianity's message might be the same the world over, but its presentation can vary widely. Witness the novel approach taken by Father Miguel Raiz, 61, of Barcelona in his denunciation of the evils of lust and fornication. Anxious to impress upon his elderly congregation the inherent wickedness of 'seething bodily desire', Father Raiz had assembled an outlandish

Sunday morning collection of erotic aids in his church, laying them out on top of his pulpit and vigorously demonstrating each one prior to dropping it into a flaming dustbin. Worshippers watched in horror as he flagellated the lectern, waved crotchless underpants in the air and activated a massive, battery-powered dildo, which he left wriggling around on the altar 'like an electric cucumber'. The climax came when a life-sized rubber woman, inflated with a special oxygen tank, exploded after being crammed into the flaming bin, showering scalding latex over the congregation and igniting an old woman in the front row. 'God's wrath was plain to see,' thundered Father Raiz.

Probably the most reprehensible class of thief, other than those who work for the Inland Revenue, comprises the ones who steal from places of worship. Even for atheists there is something particularly loathsome about theft from a holy site. That said, churches do appear to have their own inbuilt defence mechanism – a sort of divine watch scheme – as discovered by American burglar Stephen Millar, who spent three days trapped beneath a half-ton statue of the Virgin Mary. Mr Millar, 16, of Connecticut was in the process of robbing a local chapel when divine retribution struck. 'I'd just cleared the altar and drunk all the communion wine,' he explained, 'when I saw the statue in a corner. It was a huge thing with long blonde hair and beautiful blue eyes, like Sharon Stone. I don't know why, but I thought, "Come on, let's have a dance," so I hugged it and then it fell on me.' Despite repeated cries for help and earnest repetition of the Lord's Prayer, Mr Millar remained trapped beneath the statue for almost 70 hours, until he was discovered by a cleaner who sprayed him in the face with polish and called the police. 'God don't take no shit!' said the contrite kleptomaniac.

Don't let their wimples fool you! On the surface they might look caring and gentle, but when they lose their temper nuns are a force to be reckoned with, as demonstrated in Italy, where a frail 70-year-old Ursuline nun 'beat the living crap' out of a man she caught stealing from her collection box. Sister Maria Rosaria of Brindisi was dusting in a corner of her church when she spotted six-foot-three thug Alberto Piccatto helping himself to money from the collection box. 'The old bird went totally batshit,' explained Piccatto from his hospital bed. 'She screamed, "I spy a greedy boy!" and poked me in the eye with a giant candle.' As the cringing criminal stumbled into some chairs, Sister Maria then tried to strangle him with a broom before hitting him over the head with a large leather-bound Bible and stabbing him in the buttock with a six-foot iron candle snuffer. 'Baby Jesus came to me,' she later explained, 'and said "Attack!" '

Although one of the most aesthetically pleasing of religions, Judaism can also be one of the most frustrating, as discovered by an Israeli family who were forced to watch their flat burn down because Sabbath rules prevented them from calling the fire brigade. When their kitchen caught fire, the Aron family of Tel Aviv immediately consulted a local rabbi as to whether they could break the Sabbath observance and phone for a fire engine. The rabbi considered the problem for 30 minutes, consulting various books of law and praying for divine guidance, eventually deciding that they could phone for help, by which time the flat had been completely gutted. 'I kept telling him time was running out,' said the horrified homeowner, 'but he just said, "God doesn't wear an Accurist," which you can't really argue with.'

At the risk of incurring a fatwah and spending the rest of my life playing cribbage with Salman Rushdie, it has to be said that certain aspects of Islam are patently baffling. Nowhere more so than in Egypt, where Muslim extremists have demanded the destruction of a landmark tower because it looks like a penis. The 617-foot Cairo tower, in the heart of Egypt's capital, is, it appears, a constant architectural temptation to Egyptian women, not least because the trees surrounding it resemble nothing so much as 'the tufting, frond-like hair of a grown man's private parts'. Even more outrageous, however, is the fact that, when viewed from certain quarters in particularly clear weather, the tower appears to be flanked by two domes 'like giant shiny testicles'. 'It is against sharia law and must fall!' thundered one Al-Jihad spokesman. Moderates, however, are more sceptical. 'You'd have to be pretty desperate to get turned on by 600 feet of drab, ill-constructed concrete,' opined one journalist.

Bottom

You could use many adjectives to describe British Rail, but 'charismatic' is probably not one of them. Not so the Indian rail service, which numbers, amongst its tens of thousands of employees, a certain Mr Rajiv Kumar, recently disciplined for publicly breaking wind to the tune of Beethoven's Fifth Symphony (in D minor). Mr Kumar, 37, of Madras has become something of a legend at his local station, to which people have been known to travel from miles around solely to experience his novel forays into the world of customer entertainment. Past spectaculars have included a dramatic exhibition of spoon playing over the station's public address system, belly-dancing in the ticket office and snake-charming in the toilets, the latter having to be abandoned after a man was bitten by a cobra whilst washing his feet. Breaking wind to Beethoven, however, was Mr Kumar's *pièce de résistance*. 'I like to entertain people,' explained the anarchic announcer. 'I often fart at parties and everyone loves it, so I thought, why not at work?' Unfortunately, the rail authorities were less than impressed, branding the performance 'a disgusting deviation from the correct timetable' and sacking the unfortunate Mr Kumar on the spot. 'Perhaps I should have done it to Chris de Burgh instead,' he reflected.

One of the more traumatic experiences that most of us undergo at some point or another – often at several points if we fail the first time – is the driving test. Few test candidates, however, can have had as miserable a time of it as American Ebony Frew of Cleveland, who as well as having to perform a series of intricate and complex manoeuvres had to contend with an examiner who kept breaking wind. According to Miss Frew, 24, the man had barely got into the car before he clutched the dashboard, lifted his leg and 'guffed like a bison'. This, however, was merely a prelude, the next 30 minutes being punctuated by an exotic selection of 'peeps, parps and hoots', so that by the time the unfortunate woman came to do her emergency stop she was 'half-unconscious' and crashed into the back of a fruit van. 'I told him what the problem was,' explained Miss Frew, 'but he just said, "You're mistaken, young lady, it was exhaust fumes," and then he failed me.' She has since flunked the test on a further six occasions. 'Flatulence has ruined my life,' she confessed.

Bad weather, terrorists, technical problems, sickness – there is a wide variety of reasons why planes are occasionally forced to make emergency landings. Pig flatulence, however, has never figured highly on the causal list of midair crises – until, that is, a South African plane almost crashed at Gatwick because wind from its cargo of 72 pigs set off fire alarms. Trouble started when passengers and crew on the flight from London to Johannesburg noticed an unpleasant smell pervading the cabin. 'I was eating my chicken supreme with baby new potatoes and cauliflower florettes when I became aware of a stench,' said one passenger. 'At first I thought it was the old lady beside me, so I leant over and said politely, "Farted?" but she misheard me and said, "No thank you, I'll have the treacle pudding." Then all the fire alarms went off.' The plane was forced to make an emergency landing at Gatwick, where it was discovered that methane emissions from the pigs in the hold had reached dangerous levels. 'It was a time bomb just waiting to blow off,' said one airline official. 'I should never have given them damp oats for breakfast,' admitted the pigs' owner contritely.

If you find buying clothes embarrassing, just thank your lucky stars you've never had to buy them from Simeon Beep, an Australian tailor who exacted a terrible revenge after a customer allegedly broke wind in one of his suits.

Thirty-year-old executive Brian Cahill of Perth was trying on a most becoming sky-blue, double-breasted pinstripe suit in Beep's shop when the latter belligerently accused him of 'gassing off'. Cahill vigorously denied the charge, but Beep insisted he had heard an 'extremely loud fart, a Krakatoa of a fart' and that Cahill would now have to purchase the suit. After a long and heated altercation, Beep calmed down and Cahill returned to work, believing the matter closed. An hour later, however, he was conducting an interview when Beep's voice, amplified by a megaphone, wafted upwards from the office car park, announcing that 'Cahill farts in clean cotton suits and doesn't wash his bottom'. The trumpeting tailor was eventually dragged away by police, but remains unrepentant. 'Farters like that are a menace to decent society,' he opined.

One of the most courageous, not to mention malodorous, attempts to enter *The Guinness Book of Records* was made by 27-year-old Kenyan bus driver Moses Kwigezi, who undertook to wear the same underpants – 24 hours a day – for a record-breaking five years. 'The name of the game is not to move around too much,' explained the rancid record-chaser. 'The stiller you remain, the greater the chance of your knickers retaining their integrity over a period of years.' Buoyed up by his own advice, Mr Kwigezi began his quest in 1993, putting on his underpants before a huge crowd of supporters and posing for photographs. All went well for the first three years, with the dark-blue heavy-weave cotton panties showing few signs of mould or disintegration. It was at the beginning of year four, however, that things went disastrously wrong when Mr Kwigezi's long-suffering bus passengers finally rioted, dragging him into the road, stripping him naked and ritually burning his record-breaking underpants. 'He stank,' said one anonymous attacker. 'Even at the back of the bus, with the windows open and a perfumed handkerchief held over your nose, it was still hell on earth.' Although saddened by the violent end to his record attempt, Mr Kwigezi remains philosophical. 'I thought pants were my route to fame,' he mused, 'but it was not to be. Now I am trying to wear a pair of red leather gloves for an entire decade.'

Toilets can be extremely hazardous places, as discovered by New Yorker Richard Stern, who was recently rushed to hospital with a broken pelvis after being sucked down his lavatory. The incident was, it appears, the latest in a series of unprovoked attacks by the belligerent privy, which Mr Stern believes is haunted by the ghost of a plumber who suffered a fatal heart attack whilst mending it. 'It was about two years ago,' remembers Mr Stern. 'He was doing something to the U-bend when suddenly there was a loud thud. I thought maybe he'd had an accident with the toilet brush so I ran in and there he was, dead, with his head wedged against the toilet-roll holder.' Ever since, according to Mr Stern, his lavatory has been behaving badly. 'It whispers the plumber's name when I'm trying to sleep,' he explains, 'and whenever I go to the loo the man's face appears in the pan and screams, "It's going to be a bad one!" after which water sprays in my face and the pipes clank.' The tormented lavatory-goer is convinced the haunting is because he didn't give the plumber a tip, although his doctor has a slightly less flattering explanation: 'The guy is a grade-one sultana fruitcake.'

One doesn't normally associate trips to the toilet with extreme heroism, but an exception must be made in the case of Kenyan Zgabe Hoto, who displayed bravery of the first order whilst sitting on the second-class toilet of the Nairobi to Mombasa express. Mr Hoto, 40, a structural engineer, had settled himself on the lavatory and was reading a technical pamphlet when he suddenly felt 'cold water lapping around my buttocks like caressing hands'. Realising the lavatory was flooding, Mr Hoto, with admirable presence of mind and total disregard for his own comfort, squeezed his legs together, gripped the lavatory seat and pulled hard 'so I was wedged in the hole and no water could get out'. He remained thus for almost nine hours, singing hymns to keep up his spirits and telling fellow passengers 'to go away because I am engaged on important business'. Guards, meanwhile, brought him honey cakes and coffee, whilst his wife massaged his legs to stop them going numb. When the train finally pulled into Mombasa, dozens of passengers lined the platform and cheered an exhausted Mr Hoto as he was stretchered to a waiting ambulance. 'If it wasn't for him the whole carriage would have been flooded,' said a grateful railway spokesman. 'He is a brave man, and a Christian.'

It's bad enough being robbed, but when the robber compounds his crime by abusing your lavatory you know for sure that you're cursed. Such was certainly the opinion of Canadian store-owner Gerbert Huck, who suffered the indignity not only of being raided but of having a malodorous stench left in his toilet to boot. Mr Huck was serving customers in his shop in Vernon, British Columbia, when thief Egbert Spruce, 40, ran in with a gun and cried, 'This is a robbery!' Barely had the raid begun, however, before the pistol-toting Mr Spruce felt 'a stirring of the bowels' and realised it was 'dump or die time'. He therefore instructed customers and staff to wait with their hands up while he availed himself of the on-site toilet facilities. Amazingly they complied, listening to a succession of groans and plops and even bringing him a new, extra-soft toilet roll when he requested it. 'We thought he might be looking at us through the keyhole,' explained Mr Huck. 'The last thing you want to do is upset a thief whilst he's on the toilet.' After 20 minutes Mr Spruce re-emerged – looking, according to eyewitnesses, 'about a stone lighter' – and duly completed the robbery. 'It was particularly upsetting because he didn't even pull the chain,' moaned a distraught Mr Huck.

One's ability to hide from the police is dictated by a variety of factors – intelligence, adeptness at disguise, the number of people who are prepared to help you. One quality above all others, however, helps in the battle to avoid detection: smallness. The smaller you are, the harder it is to find you, as demonstrated by master criminal Theos Karamani, a Greek midget who gave police the slip by flushing himself down a toilet. Following a botched jewellery raid three-foot-four Mr Karamani had rushed into a small restaurant with the police in hot pursuit. An extensive search of the premises, however, failed to reveal any sign of the diminutive villain. 'It was like he disappeared into thin air,' said one officer. 'We pulled up all the floorboards, and even dug up the garden, but he was nowhere to be seen.' Eventually, convinced their quarry had somehow escaped over the rooftops, the search was called off, although not before policeman Nikolas Panotis had popped into the lavatory to relieve himself. Here, on lifting the toilet lid, he discovered what he initially took to be 'toilet paper with spiders on it', but then, to his amazement, realised was actually the elusive jewel thief curled up in the lavatory bowl, 'like a little dragon'. The latter at first claimed he was a plumber 'doing complex repairs', but after Panotis had pulled the chain three times he admitted to his crimes and was arrested. 'We are all flushed with success,' said one senior policeman.

There have been numerous instances of people dying whilst sitting on the toilet. It would appear, however, that 21-year-old Mr Kitano Koshiki of

Tokyo is the only person who has died whilst bowing to one. Mr Koshiki was waiting for an interview at a major Tokyo bank when the tragedy occurred. Having arrived early for his meeting, he had taken refuge in a lavatory cubicle, where it seems that he was practising how best to greet his interviewer. 'We were using the urinals,' explained one bank employee, 'when we heard a soft voice saying, "Thank you, dear sir, I am honoured to be in your presence." Then there was a sort of rustling sound, as of someone bowing, which was repeated many times until there was a loud clank and a thump like a body falling to the floor.' After their calls of 'Are you all right?' went unanswered, the bank employees alerted security guards, who broke into the toilet and discovered a recumbent Mr Koshiki draped across the lavatory with a shattered skull. 'He died in a bank, which is as he would have wanted it,' said Mr Koshiki's tearful mother.

Whatever else you might think about the Japanese, they are certainly one of the most honest races on earth. Where else would a 19-year-old student find £122,000 in a public lavatory, spend half a day walking up and down a street asking passers-by if the money belonged to them and then hand it in to the police? Not in Peckham, you can be sure. Maths scholar Kando Kenasaki had spotted the money in a brown paper bag whilst sitting on the toilet in a suburb of Tokyo. 'Initially I thought it might be some sort of novelty lavatory paper,' he admitted, 'but when I saw it was real I stood on the toilet and asked the people in the cubicles on either side if they had lost a lot of money. They said no, however, and told me to leave them alone.' Having put his trousers back on and washed his hands, Mr Kenasaki proceeded to ask the occupants of other cubicles if the money was theirs, but all answered in the negative and he was eventually thrown out by the lavatory attendant, who thought he was soliciting. Thereafter he spent an entire afternoon offering the money to pedestrians, but when no one would take it, he handed it in at a local police station. The story doesn't end there, however, because after extensive investigations the police proved equally unable to locate the money's rightful owner and it was therefore given back to its finder. 'I go to the public lavatory every day,' said Mr Kenasaki, 'but apart from one man who offered to give me a massage, no one has so far claimed it.'

That's Entertainment

The life of an actor can be a desperate one. Low wages, years out of work, a constant stream of auditions and rejections – it is, in many ways, a form of vocational torture. Few performers, however, even at their lowest and most dispirited ebb, can have gone so far to secure work as Mr Luther Charles, who cut off his ears to land a role in a play about singing missionaries. Mr Charles, 41, had been out of work for almost five years when he spotted an advert in an actor's magazine for 'Genuine earless performers'. Being desperate for employment, and seemingly condemned to a life of penurious inactivity, he decided 'to go for it' and, having drunk a bottle of whisky and numbed them with a block of ice, removed both the specified appendages with a hacksaw. He duly arrived at the audition, bandaged but confident, only to be informed that the magazine had made a printing error and the advert should actually have read 'Genuine fearless performers'. He is now undergoing psychiatric treatment after insisting he is a reincarnation of Pharaoh Rameses II.

One of the great figures in Filipino cabaret is singer Spangle Kwok, who has provided the entertainment at the bizarrely named Jellied Monster Bar in Manila for the last 14 years. During all of that time the management and clientele have only ever allowed him to sing two songs – 'Stairway to Heaven' and 'The Girl from Ipanema' – which he repeats over and over again, sometimes as many as 10 times each per night. In 1987 he tried to expand his repertoire to include a cover version of Abba's 'Dancing Queen', but was bottled off stage, whilst an experimental performance combining the lyrics of 'Stairway to Heaven' with the music from 'The Girl from Ipanema' resulted in Mr Kwok being attacked by the audience and hospitalised. Eventually he decided enough was enough and attempted to escape to another country, but he was spotted at Manila docks and carried back in time for the evening show. Mr Kwok has now resigned himself to spending the rest of his career at the Jellied Monster, although he has got exciting plans for the year 2000 – 'My Way' with bagpipes.

Being small is not always a disadvantage, especially when it comes to limbo-dancing competitions. Witness events in Brazil, where Mr Hector Basoles, proprietor of the Rising Moon Club in São Paulo, is seeking to ban midgets from his weekly limbo-dancing competition because they keep winning it. The worst offender, it seems, is three-foot-two Luis Guimares, who has walked – or limboed – away with the £50 top prize for the last eight weeks running. 'He comes in dressed in a gold lamé smock and all the competitors groan because they know they haven't got a chance,' said an angry Mr Basoles. 'He can practically walk under the pole. It's not fair. And now he's started bringing in his friends, and they're all tiny too, so that suddenly Monday night is midget night. It's costing me a fortune in prize money.' The concerned club-owner is now seeking a court order to ban Mr Guimares and his friends from the club, 'until such time as they undertake not to enter the limbo competition, or else get bigger'. 'I was prepared to let it go,' explained Mr Basoles. 'but when my wife found two of them asleep in her laundry basket I knew things had gone too far.'

Few countries come up with such bizarre, dangerous and utterly compulsive game shows as Japan, and few Japanese game shows are as bizarre, dangerous and utterly compulsive as *Drink Till You Drop*, the show currently topping the ratings in the Land of the Rising Sun. The essence of the programme is contained within the title, with competitors from a variety of backgrounds imbibing as much alcohol as they possibly can within the space of an hour, this in the hope of winning a car, or a holiday, or a cash lump sum. The results can be highly unpredictable, although it is but rarely the show descends into the chaos witnessed when a group of female contestants went completely out of control. 'It was the crème de menthe, advocaat and shampoo cocktails that did it,' explained a shocked audience member. 'One of the women was sick all over the camera, and then tried to make us chant "Up the arse!" but we booed her and slapped her with our programmes.' This was just the start, however, as another woman wet herself, two attacked a cameraman before stripping down to their underwear and doing the cancan, and one passed out. All five women were later hospitalised with acute alcohol poisoning. 'They acted like drunkards!' said the show's incensed producer.

One of the most exciting, not to mention shocking, game shows of recent years was Taiwan's *Electric Fingers*. The concept of the show was simplicity itself. Competitors were asked a series of increasingly difficult general knowledge questions, each correct answer taking them a step nearer the $20,000 grand prize. Incorrect responses, however, resulted in a hefty electric shock, administered via brightly coloured electrodes taped to the fingers. Each burst of voltage sparked frenzied audience reaction, with things really hotting up during a free-for-all round in which contestants were allowed to administer shocks to their opponents or, for bonus points, themselves. Many contestants passed out with the pain, although, in a bitterly ironical twist to the whole thing, the only known fatality was a man who suffered a heart attack when he won the grand prize. 'He looked like he'd been struck by lightning,' said the show's producer.

One of the most charismatic, and certainly the worst, television weather forecasters of all time was India's Cibonco Mala. Whereas most forecasters get it wrong occasionally, Mr Mala, 56, made a virtue of getting it wrong with every single prediction he made. Drought warnings coincided with floods in which 400 people were killed, whilst an augury of deadly frosts resulted in a six-month heatwave. 'He was absolutely, unbelievably terrible,' admitted Mr Mala's producer. 'It got to the point where his forecasts were so inaccurate they were almost accurate.' The unfortunate presenter was regularly pelted with donkey droppings, and was once attacked by a man who had spent his entire life's savings on an inflatable life raft after Mala erroneously predicted a hurricane. His career reached its climax during a live broadcast when cameramen started blowing raspberries at him and chanting, 'Snow brain!' whereupon Mr Mala assaulted the cameras with his pointing-stick and screamed, 'I hope it rains piss!' He was wrestled to the floor by technical staff and now runs a sweetshop in Bombay.

The degrading world of hard-core pornography produces few heroes, but if anyone deserves the title it is 46-year-old Polish librarian Simon Skara. Mr Skara, a myopic 17-stone social misfit, had purchased a hard-core sex video, coyly entitled *Thirsty Nuns Go Berserk*, from Warsaw's red light district. He was on his way home with his prize, 'trembling with excitement', when he spotted a policeman standing at the end of his street. 'I'd never bought a dirty film before and I panicked,' he explained. 'I thought, "Oh, God, they're going to arrest me and tell mother," so I ran away as fast as I could and took sanctuary in the forest.' Here he remained in hiding for 13 days, living off roots and berries and drinking from a stream, until eventually, half dead from cold and hunger, he gave himself up at the local police station. 'He burst in, all muddy and covered with leaves, and screamed, "Yes, yes, I am the man with the disgusting film. Dear God have mercy on my soul," ' said one police officer. 'He then went down on his knees and begged us not to tell his mother, who is a Catholic and a leading Rotary Club member.' Much to Mr Skara's surprise, however, the policemen informed him that he wasn't a wanted man and that porn wasn't illegal, before inquiring whether they might have a look at the film on the station video machine. 'We put it on and sat back in anticipation,' explained Mr Skara, 'but then my heart sank. No nuns, no thirst, no one going berserk, just two old men singing folk songs. With tambourines.'

With his homely, cuboid post van and trusty, black and white cat, cartoon hero Postman Pat is the last person you'd imagine to be involved in the world of organised crime. Appearances can be deceptive, however; or at least Japanese petty crook Wang Woo thought so, throwing himself from a ten-storey building under the mistaken belief that his son's Postman Pat video contained subliminal threats from ruthless Yakuza gangsters. The tragic mix-up occurred because, by an unfortunate coincidence, Postman Pat has only three fingers, a feature shared by the Japanese Yakuza Mafia, who are required to amputate a digit to demonstrate loyalty to their organisation. According to his wife, Mr Woo, 36, of Tokyo went 'white as a boiled oyster' as soon as the video – which had been bought in England – came on, screaming, 'The bastards have found me at last!' and cowering behind a sofa with a cushion over his head. Each time Postman Pat waved at the camera, 'He squealed like a piglet,' and finally, when the animated mailman reached into his post bag, cried, 'I know what's in there, arsehole!' and launched himself through the living-room window, tumbling to his death 100 feet below. Pat's creators have now agreed to draw him an extra finger prior to video distribution in the Far East.

Every Christmas throws up its fair share of drunken Santas, rude Santas and Santas doing weird things, but there has, it appears, only ever been one rude, drunken, nude, parachuting Santa, and that was Chester Snope of Pratt, Kansas. The original idea was that 18-stone Mr Snope, disguised as Santa Claus and accompanied by two midgets dressed as little green pixies, would parachute into the centre of town as the climax to a day of Yuletide festivities. According to his pixies, however, Mr Snope, 41, had been drinking heavily beforehand – 'At least 26 Budweisers and a bottle of bourbon' was one estimate – and as soon as he jumped from the plane and his parachute opened, he began to remove his trousers, pants and red fur booties. 'We saw this enormous bottom in the sky,' said one onlooker, 'with two pixies trying to cover it up with their pixie hats. Then he crashed into a candy-floss machine and passed out.' The emergency services arrived within minutes, but attempts to remove Mr Snope were hampered by hordes of hysterical children demanding a look at 'Santa's bum'.

The fundamental problem with modern art, aside from the fact that most of it isn't very good, is that you can never be quite sure what's art and what isn't. Such was certainly the experience of sanitation expert Bill Biggins, who was arrested at a chic New York gallery after inadvertently eating a sculpture. Mr Biggins, 51, was visiting the gallery with his wife when the accident happened. Whilst his spouse wandered around admiring the exhibits, Mr Biggins had sat down on a podium, where he discovered a heap of tasty-looking sugar doughnuts. 'I thought someone might have left them there by accident,' he explained, 'but when no one came to claim them I thought, "Bugger this!" and tucked in. They were rather stale, but the jam was lovely.' There were eight doughnuts in the pile, all of which Mr Biggins devoured, and it was only when two security guards rushed at him and wrestled him to the floor that the voracious visitor realised his impromptu snack was actually a ground-breaking work of modern art entitled *Nude Greek Boys Dancing*. 'He offered to sick it up for us,' said the gallery owner, 'but vomit simply couldn't convey the sense of classical beauty inherent in the doughnut original.'

Planes, Trains and Automobiles

Ongoing efforts to improve the safety of air travel have not been helped by African air traffic controller Luther Ungumbe, who nearly caused a major accident by doing his tap-dance practice in the control tower. Mr Ungumbe, 41, was in sole charge of the tower, at a rural airport in Mozambique, when the incident occurred. 'I radioed the tower and said I was coming in for landing,' explained pilot Christian Kaget, 'but all I could hear was a sort of tapping sound. I said, "Is this interference?" but the sound just got louder, and then a voice said, "Yeh, man, feet on springs!" That's when I contacted the airport authorities.' Officials rushed to the tower, where they discovered Mr Ungumbe, in a pair of patent red tap-shoes, dancing on a desk. 'I said, "What the hell are you doing?" ' recalled the airport manager, 'and he said, "Something by Sammy Davis Junior." So we arrested him.' The cavorting controller has since been dismissed. It later transpired that he was practising for a charity event in aid of the families of two men killed in a flying accident.

There are few things more off-putting on a long train journey than being stuck opposite someone who picks their nose. Few of us, however, would take such direct action as Texan Wendell Snuck, currently serving three years in prison after throwing a man from a moving railway carriage for 'staring at the snot in his hanky'. Six-foot-six evangelist Mr Snuck had become 'enraged with the rage of the just' when fellow traveller Andrew Carr repeatedly sneezed into his handkerchief and then looked at what had come out. 'He kept peering at it and licking his lips,' explained a disgusted Mr Snuck. 'Then he poked it with his finger and stirred it about, like it was stew or something.' Mr Snuck eventually lost control when Carr placed his finger in his mouth and sucked it 'like a lollipop', picking him up 'as though he were a rag doll' and pushing him out of the train window. 'Mucus is of the devil,' Snuck later explained. 'God gave us noses and Lucifer in his wickedness filled them with slime.'

Passengers are always leaving things on trains. Umbrellas, wallets, bags, items of clothing – you name it, it's been left. There are, however, but few instances of travellers forgetting actual bodily parts when disembarking at the end of their journey. One such case occurred in Egypt, where a young man inadvertently abandoned his head on top of a train. The discarded bonce, sporting a Walkman personal stereo and black baseball cap, was initially spotted by a policeman at Cairo station who noticed blood on the carriage windows. 'At first I thought it was decorations, to brighten up the train and attract customers,' explained Sergeant Abdul Sedi, 'so I shouted, "Hooray! Hooray! Very colourful! Very nice!" But then I saw the head on the roof and knew immediately that all was not well.' After some discussion, the bloodstained cranium was poked down with a long bamboo pole and shown to passengers. When no one claimed it, however, it was consigned to a fridge in the lost property office, where it remained amongst the onions and cans of Coca-Cola for three days until its missing body was discovered beneath a low-level bridge 60 miles away. 'I remember someone once left 18 watermelons on a train,' said one official. 'Railway work can be very exciting.'

If ever Ford plan an advertising campaign to promote the interior spaciousness of their vehicles, they would be mad not to feature Mr John Ofosu, who holds the all-time record for the number of goats in T-shirts one can cram into the back of a Ford Escort. Mr Ofosu, 32, of Ghana was recently stopped by traffic police with no fewer than 14 pregnant goats in his car. It appears that he had been stealing the creatures from roadside villages and then disguising them as members of his family in order to avoid detection. 'I was manning a roadblock when the accused pulled up in his car,' explained police sergeant Abel Kanawi. 'He wound down the window and said, "Just out for a family drive! Nice weather for it!" I thought at first his wife and children were dreadfully deformed and said, "I'm so sorry." But then I saw they were goats in Michael Jackson T-shirts so I arrested him.' Mr Ofosu is now serving a prison sentence for theft and 'unnatural practices'. 'You see some funny things on the road,' said Sergeant Kanawi. 'I once stopped a man with almost 6,000 onions in his car.'

Some motorists have no consideration whatsoever for cyclists. One such is French driver Cecille Pork, who sped for eight miles with a mountain-biker spread-eagled across her windscreen, all the while refusing to stop because she thought he was a mugger. Madame Pork, 83, had already been banned from driving once for running over a librarian whom she mistook for a large traffic bollard. On this particular occasion she was driving out of her home town of Valence when she crashed into a cyclist at a crossroads, catapulting the unfortunate man on to her bonnet, where he clung for dear life whilst the outrageous octogenarian accelerated to 70 mph. 'She was jabbing at the window and shouting, "Murderer! Murderer!"' recalled the victim. 'I screamed, "For God's sake, woman, I'm a cyclist," but she just hooted her horn and turned the windscreen wipers on.' Despite the man's pleas and the gesticulating of other motorists, Madame Pork continued determinedly on her way, coming to a halt only when she was forced into a field by three police cars. Despite receiving a life ban, she remained unrepentant. 'My only regret,' she later declared, 'is that I didn't drive into a wall and squash him like a chocolate truffle.'

Whilst most hit and run drivers deserve every torment society can possibly heap upon them, there is the odd exception. One of these must certainly be Chicago motorist Betheny Sluce, who spent two years in hiding after running over a little girl in a remote country lane. Miss Sluce was returning from a weekend with friends when the incident occurred. 'I was coming round a corner when this little girl ran into the road,' she remembered tearfully. 'I hit her full on and she went flying over the car. I'll never forget her white face and funny teeth, and the terrible screaming she made.' A hysterical Miss Sluce failed to stop her car. Instead she drove home, where she packed a bag, emptied her savings account and moved to Texas, thereafter spending the next two years living under a pseudonym. 'I know it was wrong not to stop,' she said, 'but I just couldn't face the shame.' Eventually, however, overcome with remorse and a need for atonement, she returned to Chicago and gave herself up to the police, informing them, 'I killed the girl. Now take me to the electric chair.' To her surprise, however, there was no record of a hit and run on the date she gave, and it eventually transpired, after some investigation, that the victim had not been a little girl at all, but rather a goat wearing a dress and bonnet as part of a local agricultural festival. 'Which just goes to show, you should always stop and see who you've run over,' said a rejuvenated Miss Sluce.

There is an almost endless list of factors which can cause road accidents. Amongst the obvious ones, however, such as drunkenness, adverse weather conditions and speeding, one hazard has been almost entirely overlooked – yodelling. Witness events in Switzerland, where a strenuous bout of musical ululation resulted in a mass pile-up just north of the town of Thun. At the centre of the disaster were octogenarian couple Maurice and Sacha Weedsnout.

The doddery day-trippers, 83 and 80 respectively, were enjoying an afternoon out in their car when Mr Weedsnout turned on the radio, tuning into an easy-listening music station which was presenting a selection of great yodelling hits. 'It was so uplifting,' admitted Mrs Weedsnout, 'I said, "Shall we join in, Maurice?" and he said, "Yes, my dear, we shall." So we did.' Initially the couple sang along calmly, but as the show built to a crescendo so the elderly enthusiasts became increasingly excited, yodelling at the tops of their voices and slapping the dashboard with their hands. 'We were singing "My Goat, My Goat, My Little Mountain Goat",' explained Mrs Weedsnout, 'when Maurice took his hands off the wheel and tried to clap them behind his head, which is when he lost control.' The Weedsnouts' car veered across the road, crashing into a fruit stall and causing a 13-car pile-up. 'It's lucky they didn't play "The Spinning Milkmaid",' said Mr Weedsnout, 'or we could really have been in trouble.'

Academics might be light-years ahead of us mere mortals in the brain department, but when it comes to simple things like popping round the corner to visit a relative they get horribly confused. Witness German professor Nestor Tribulus, whose brief drive down the road to visit his sister Piminy turned into a 600-mile odyssey through Eastern Europe. Mr Tribulus, 79, of Munich, lived only 500 yards from his sister's bungalow, yet on his way there somehow contrived to take a wrong turning and ended up on an autobahn. 'I thought it was a new one-way system,' he explained, 'so I just kept going. I was aware it was taking longer to get to Piminy's than usual, but thought that was a small price to pay for industrial progress.' After three hours of driving he crossed into Czechoslovakia – mistaking the border checkpoint for a drive-in shopping centre – and from thence into Poland, all the while cursing the influx of foreigners that made Germans 'feel like strangers in their own country'. Eventually he crossed back into Germany, arriving home some 15 hours after setting out. 'Next time she can come to me for tea,' he later commented.

Whatever you might say about women drivers, at least they are more responsible than men. Responsibility takes on a whole new meaning, however, when it comes to Ms Chrysanthemum Choo, arguably the world's safest ever motorist. Ms Choo, 30, of Miami had returned to her car after a shopping expedition, starting the engine and patiently waited for an opportunity to pull out on to the main road. Eight hours later she was still patiently waiting. 'I like to be careful,' she explained. 'There were many cars around and I didn't want to do anything rash.' Things quietened down considerably during the night, but unfortunately by that point Ms Choo had fallen asleep, waking up just in time for the morning rush hour. It was another four hours before the desperate driver eventually saw her chance. Overcome with relief she slammed her foot on the accelerator and sped on to the road – straight into the side of a passing police car. 'I obviously wasn't careful enough,' she admitted.

Nothing is more annoying than parking your car in a car park and then returning to discover you can't remember where you've left it. Imagine how elderly French couple René and Lucille Schubelle felt, therefore, when they returned from a shopping expedition to discover that not just their car but the entire car park had disappeared. Mr and Mrs Schubelle, both 84, of Calais had left their Renault Clio in 'one of those new-fangled municipal parking garages' on the seafront. When they came back two hours later, however, laden down with shopping, they were surprised to discover that the entire car park had vanished into thin air. Thinking perhaps it was 'something to do with Arab terrorists', they contacted the police, who, after a brief investigation, discovered that what the Schubelles had taken to be a multistorey car park was in fact the car deck of a cross-Channel ferry. 'When we told them their car had gone to England they got very confused,' said one official. 'They seemed to think it was a punishment for having a dirty windscreen.'

For most of us a bed or a couch will do just fine. Some, however, prefer to sleep in more exotic places, one such being inveterate Australian party-goer Billy Snout, who snoozed peacefully on top of a car whilst being driven at 70 mph through the streets of Sydney. Mr Snout, 19, was at a friend's birthday party when the incident occurred. Having drunk 'a ridiculous amount of vodka' and smoked some cannabis, Mr Snout decided it was time for bed, duly staggering into a pitch-dark bedroom, stripping naked, clambering into a bunk bed and passing out. What he didn't know, however, was that the 'bedroom' was actually the garage of the house and the 'bunk bed' the roof rack of his friend's car. 'I woke up and everything was whizzing round and round, and there were lots of flashing lights,' explained the sozzled stowaway, 'but I thought it was just the booze, so I dropped off again.' The car's four occupants were only alerted to the presence of their unexpected passenger when a shower of sick spattered all over the windscreen. 'We pulled in to the kerb and found him leaning over the edge of the roof rack being sick,' said the shocked driver. 'I said, "My God, Billy, how long have you been there?" But he just farted and told me to turn the lights out.'

Every taxi driver has a horror story to tell, although few could match that of Kenyan cabbie Nelson Sacope, who was forced to drive for two days with a gun to his head by an old woman who wanted to see some elephants. Barely had 76-year-old Frenchwoman Marie Colombe climbed into Mr Sacope's car outside Mombasa airport than she produced a pistol and ordered the dumbfounded driver, 'Take me to the elephants!' There ensued a bizarre 48-hour odyssey around Kenya with only the odd stop for petrol, which Mr Sacope was forced to pay for out of his own pocket. 'We saw every beast God made,' said the distressed cabbie, 'flamingos, giraffes, crocodiles. Everything except elephants. She was getting more and more agitated and kept screaming, "Have you eaten them, you greedy boy?" It was terrible.' Eventually Mrs Colombe asked to be returned to Mombasa airport, where she gave her driver £1.30 and a banana for his trouble and then disappeared into the departure lounge. She was later arrested boarding a flight to France, although magistrates freed her after she insisted she was Tarzan's estranged love child.

Bulgaria has, in its time, produced the very best and the very worst of bus drivers. In the former category must be included Zoltan Szabich, a man of such innate dedication to his craft that he insisted on completing his route despite suffering a massive heart attack midway through. Although paralysed down the left side, virtually blind and unable to breathe properly, Mr Szabich gamely told his passengers he was feeling 'fresh as a juicy beetroot' and continued to drive until he had dropped everyone off. At quite the other end of the dedication scale, however, comes driver Milosch Pob, a man of spellbinding irresponsibility, who thought nothing of abandoning a busload of passengers in order to indulge in some hanky-panky with his girlfriend. On the day in question Mr Pob, 31, had already caused considerable disgruntlement by going 12 miles out of his way to visit a supermarket, taking two passengers inside with him to help carry his shopping. Having made his purchases, he returned to his route, but then made an unscheduled stop outside a block of flats and informed passengers he was popping in for some 'sausage stew' with his girlfriend. He returned an hour later, drunk and wearing a pair of women's knickers on his head, and resumed his journey. In a bizarre coda to the whole story, a policeman who later stopped the bus was attacked by irate passengers complaining that he was delaying their journey.

Great Inventions

From time immemorial mankind has fantasised about the possibility of travelling through time. Only one man, however, has actually experienced the sensation, that being American inventor Slattery Oniontoe of Dakota, builder of the world's first-ever operational time machine. Fuelled by liquid nitrogen and based on principles of quantum physics 'that simply can't be explained to normal people', Mr Oniontoe's creation took nine years to perfect before it was ready for its first test. 'I got inside and programmed it to take me to classical Rome,' explained the intrepid inventor. 'There was a huge bang and I passed out, and when I came to the whole world seemed to be on fire.' Convinced he had arrived in ancient Pompeii during the eruption of Vesuvius, Mr Oniontoe huddled in a corner screaming, 'I come in peace!' in Latin before firemen kicked down the door and carried him to safety. 'Last year he built an atom bomb out of egg boxes,' recalled the inventor's exasperated wife.

Most taxi drivers have, at one point or another, had to put up with runaway passengers. A novel solution to the problem, however, has been developed by Czech cabbie Simon Szaditz of Prague, who, in his efforts to combat fare-dodgers, has installed not only central locking in his taxi but also a high-voltage back seat. The electrically charged interior is the latest in a series of increasingly imaginative measures employed by Mr Szaditz to deal with passengers who fail to pay for their journey. 'At first I had a picture of hell in the back with a sign saying, "Pay or Burn!" ' explained the crafty cabbie, 'but no one took any notice, so I made my mother come with me on every journey, just to keep an eye on things. It was when she ran off with one of the passengers that I knew it was time to resort to voltage.' With the aid of an electrician friend, Mr Szaditz installed an electrical plate underneath the back seat which could be activated by a small switch on the dashboard. 'Now when customers get in I give them a tootle of electricity up their bottoms,' he explained proudly, 'as a warning. Then I say, very politely, "Where to, good sir or madam?"' Public reaction has, apparently, been favourable, although one man complained when Szaditz gave him a shock because his dog broke wind. 'It wasn't a big shock,' he said. 'Just enough to let him know I was annoyed.'

One of the most annoying aspects of travelling on the Underground, aside from the fact that it's dirty, smelly and the trains are always late, is people reading your newspaper over your shoulder. One man who has tackled the problem head-on is New Yorker Stanley Lemon. Fed up with fellow commuters peering at his crossword, Mr Lemon constructed a sign saying 'I'll poke out your eyes!' which he would wave at persistent offenders. When this had no effect, however, he designed a small electric cattle prod with which he would poke anyone he suspected of muscling in on his reading material. 'It's only a few volts,' he admitted. 'Not enough to kill you, but enough to make you buy your own goddamn paper.'

Forget the motor car, the computer and the aeroplane – the greatest invention of the 20th century is without doubt Mr Yasujiro Kikowo's Patent Toilet Bicycle. Although Mr Kikowo, 65, of Tokyo was already renowned as the creator of the motorised ice skate and the singing urinal, his patent toilet bicycle is, by general consent, his masterpiece. Built for comfort, and 10 years in the making, it is specially designed to aid those 'of a constipatory nature'. It looks, in every respect, like a normal bicycle save that, in place of a saddle, it has a large rubber-rimmed funnel leading to a holding cylinder discreetly concealed between the pedals. According to its creator, strenuous cycling is a 'formidable bowel loosener' and one merely has to head off into the hills for a swift 20-minute sprint 'to achieve all that nature would wish'. For those not taken by the idea of pedalling through the Quantocks without any trousers on, the resourceful Mr Kikowo has also developed an opaque plastic cycling skirt to be worn 'for relief in crowded places'. Sales of the epoch-making machine have so far been sluggish, although its inventor remains optimistic. 'It is the way forward for sewage,' he declared confidently.

One of the most significant fashion breakthroughs of the last decade occurred in Germany, where, after years of experimentation, experts have finally come up with the Holy Grail of the footwear industry – the patent sex shoe. Apparently, a selection of strategically placed nodules on the insole stimulate a sensitive area of the underfoot, exciting a sex nerve in the brain, which in turn sends blood rushing to the groin. 'It's the culmination of a lifetime's work,' enthused creator Gunther Wanger, 71, of Dortmund. 'When I put them on and walked across the workshop, I developed a quite stupendous erection. Everybody cheered and I tried to bow, but it was just too big.' So far hundreds of pairs of the shoes have been sold across Germany, although Mrs Wanger has yet to be convinced of their efficacy. 'Gunti's always getting stiff ons,' she said, 'irrespective of whether he's wearing shoes or not.'

Inventors face many hurdles on the road to greatness and acclaim. Lack of funds, technical difficulties, a disbelieving public – all play their part in making the inventor's life a hard one. Of all the problems they experience, however, one in particular can prove fatal to their endeavours – a careless wife. Witness events in Argentina, where a woman accidentally killed her inventor husband with a giant industrial cooling fan. Hector Penna, 62, had spent four years developing the 20-foot machine in his laboratory in San Julian. 'He was standing inside the fan when I came in with his leather slippers,' explained Mrs Penna. 'It was very dark, so I switched on the light. What's wrong with that?' What's wrong was that Mr Penna had wired his creation into the laboratory light socket, so that when his wife flicked the switch it was turned on and began to rotate. 'He shouted, "No, you stupid cow!" ' said an assistant, 'and was then minced into a million bits.' 'He spattered all over me,' wailed a hysterical Mrs Penna. 'I had to wipe my husband off in the shower.'

As if they didn't have enough to worry about what with the growth of Triad gangs and the colony's imminent hand-over to China, citizens in Hong Kong are now living in fear of a new menace – out of control arm-wrestling machines. Over the past few months there have, it appears, been a spate of accidents involving the machines, with injuries ranging from dislocated shoulders to one man who suffered a fractured skull and three broken ribs. The main culprit appears to be a machine called Big Bang Bong, which comprises a large pink arm with which you wrestle, 10 play levels from 'Puny Old Woman' to 'Samurai Master' and a taunting electronic voice urging you on to ever greater feats of bicep-popping masculinity. 'I selected level six,' recalled one player, 'which is the "Young Man with a Burning Desire to Succeed" level. It was very strong, and the voice kept shouting, "Come on, you pussy! Fight! Fight, pussy!" I tried to, but it was so strong, and then all my friends started chanting "Fight, pussy!" which made me lose my concentration and then it broke my arm.' Makers of the machine have now downgraded its strength capability, although the move comes too late for one victim who committed suicide after losing on the 'Puny Old Woman' level. 'He shouted, "Yes, yes, I am a weak old woman!" ' said the man's girlfriend, 'and then shot himself in the mouth. If only he'd taken my advice and played Gunfight at the OK Corral instead.'

With complex electrical gadgetry there's always a percentage risk of malfunction. Few malfunctions, however, can have been as inconvenient as that suffered by Brazilian Carlo Paia, who discovered his 'hyper-erectile mechanical penis implant' was activated whenever his wife used an item of household electrical equipment. After years of being unable to get a proper erection, Mr Paia was delighted with his implant, which guaranteed tumescence 'when and where you want it, whatever the weather'. Things started to go wrong, however, almost as soon as Mr Paia returned home from hospital. 'Regina went into the kitchen to make a milkshake,' explained the unfortunate man. 'I said, "A chocolate one would be nice," but then she turned on the food blender and Boing! up it went like a rocket. I was in agony.' The blender was immediately unplugged, but barely had Mr Paia's erection subsided when his mobile phone started ringing and 'my trousers exploded'. Eventually he was forced to switch off the electricity at the mains and sit in pitch darkness with an ice-pack on his crotch. Even then his troubles weren't over. 'I thought everything was OK,' he said, 'but then our neighbours turned on *Wheel of Fortune* and my penis practically went through the roof.'

Dog-walking, even in the local park, can be a dangerous business, as discovered by 73-year-old Beryl Fudge when she was accidentally sucked up by an out of control pooper-vacuum whilst exercising her pug Morris. The latter, it appears, was chasing a large rubber bone when he inadvertently ran into the path of a large machine cleaning dogs' mess from the pavement. 'It was a huge great thing,' recalled a tearful Mrs Fudge, 'with lots of flashing lights and a man in very tight green overalls. It vacuumed up my Morris.' The unfortunate creature was killed instantly, whereupon, according to the pooper-scooper's driver, his machine 'went completely out of control', charging at a hysterical Mrs Fudge and trying to suck her up too. Fortunately, she was slightly too big for the machine's nozzle and got wedged halfway in, whereupon passers-by rushed to her aid. 'She was screaming, "Let me go up the tube to my Morris,"' recalled one eyewitness, 'but they pulled her out and laid her on the lawn. She didn't seem too hurt, although her legs were very mucky and her stockings had been sucked off.'

Animal Magic

Other than Norman Lamont in the nude, there are few more upsetting things to find in your house than a huge black killer spider. Such was certainly the opinion of Esther Luer, 29, of California, who spent 15 hours standing stock still in a corner of her kitchen after discovering a giant arachnid in her weekly groceries. Ms Luer was unpacking her weekly shopping when she spotted the spider lurking amongst some bananas. 'It was massive, hairy and very threatening,' she explained. 'I knew immediately it was one of those venomous bird-eating spiders which I'd read about in books, and realised that if I moved I was dead. I therefore did some deep-breathing exercises and began to chant a Buddhist mantra until it went away.' This it singularly failed to do, however, sitting still on the bananas and staring at Ms Luer 'with a look of utmost evil'. Eventually, desperate for the toilet, she edged slowly backwards out of the kitchen door and then fled the house. Local authorities were alerted and experts from the local zoo brought in to deal with the problem. Only after half the neighbourhood had been evacuated, however, and the kitchen pumped full of gas, was it discovered that the venomous bird-eating spider was in fact a large black wig. 'Easy mistake to make,' said one zoologist sarcastically.

Snakes are bad enough in the wild. They're a positive menace when they get in your underwear, however, as discovered by a Danish woman who tried to smuggle 65 rare serpents into Sweden concealed inside her Wonderbra. Customs officials at Malmo had become suspicious of Helga Snoppel, 42, as soon as she stepped off the hovercraft from Copenhagen. 'I said to my colleague, "Sweet Jesus, take a look at those!"' recalled customs officer Thomas Horst. 'But then they started rippling and juddering about.' Ms Snoppel was stopped and, despite her vehement claims that she was merely experiencing muscular spasms, was subjected to a body search, whereupon it was discovered that her 38 double-D cups were crammed to overflowing with rare grass snakes, lizards and toads. 'They spilled out like entrails,' said Mr Horst. 'It was absolutely disgusting and we had to evacuate the terminal while people from the zoo came down and swept them all up.' Ms Snoppel initially claimed that the reptiles must have slithered into her bra whilst she was asleep on the hovercraft, but later changed her story and said she had found them in the hovercraft toilet and was taking them to a special reptile sanctuary. 'Curiously enough, we didn't believe her,' said one policeman.

It's not often that a thief is punished by the things he has stolen, but that's exactly what happened to American shoplifter Barry Quemby when he appropriated a pair of giant lobsters from a Boston fishmonger's. Having seized the creatures from a tank and secreted them down the front of his trousers, Mr Quemby was making his way out of the shop when, according to eyewitnesses, he was seen to double up and scream, 'Oh no, not my nob!' He then fell into a display of tinned pilchards and began furiously clawing at his crotch, all the while groaning, 'They're crunching it.' He was rushed to hospital, where the belligerent crustaceans were surgically removed, one with the castrated criminal's severed penis still clutched firmly in its claw 'like a floppy ice-cream cone'. 'The funny thing was,' said one doctor, 'that the lobsters were making this weird clucking sound, like they were laughing.'

There are numerous instances of people being attacked by sharks whilst swimming in the sea, but there is, to date, only one of someone being attacked by a shark whilst sleeping in his own bed, that being South Seas fisherman Mr Thomas Atotay. Mr Atotay, 43, and his two crewmen were on a fishing expedition near Fiji when they encountered the big-toothed bedfellow. They had moored their boat for the night in a deserted bay and were sleeping on board when a giant 12-foot shark somehow leapt on to the deck and flapped its way down into their cabin. 'I saw something big in Mr Atotay's bed,' said one of the crewmen, 'but it was dark and I thought he had found a native girl for love. They were bouncing and I watched secretly, for I like that sort of thing.' He was alerted to the true state of affairs, however, when the shark dropped on to the floor with his employer's severed head in its mouth, whereupon he picked up a club and killed the creature. 'I suspected something was wrong,' admitted the horrified crewman. 'She was bigger than most native girls and had fins.'

They might at first sight seem like sweet little things with pretty feathers and dinky legs, but if you get on the wrong side of them birds can make your life a misery. Such was certainly the experience of American postman Spender Bumble, who had a most alarming run-in with a parrot whilst on his rounds in Miami. Mr Bumble, 47, was delivering some letters to a bungalow when he heard a voice within crying, 'Help me. My wheelchair's stuck!' Thinking that perhaps an elderly person was in distress, the munificent mailman got on his knees and peered through the letter box, only to discover that the voice was in fact that of a parrot sitting on a perch in the hall. 'I said, "Shut the fuck up, bird!"' explained Mr Bumble. 'But then it flew at me and bit me on the nose.' Despite sneezing and prodding his tormentor with a pencil, Mr Bumble was unable to break its grip on his proboscis, remaining wedged against the door for almost an hour before eventually passing out. 'Even then it wouldn't let go,' he recalled. 'I fell backwards and pulled it right through the letter box. There were feathers everywhere.' He was finally freed after neighbours called a vet, but now faces a lawsuit for cruelty to animals. 'Pinklon doesn't like people who swear,' said the parrot's proud owner.

Parrots aren't the only birds with a bad attitude towards postmen. Geese, too, have wreaked their fair share of havoc on the postal service, as demonstrated by events in Moscow, where a postman nearly had his penis bitten off by an irate gander. Mailman Yvgeny Sheshenko was approaching the end of his round when he was confronted by the feathered menace in the doorway to a large tenement block. 'It was a big thing, with large flappy wings,' recalled Mr Sheshenko. 'I said, just as a joke, "Sorry, goose, nothing for you today," at which it started hissing and lunged straight at my privates.' Residents, alerted by an ear-piercing scream of, 'Oh, it will snap it off!' came rushing out to discover the pained postman crouched at the foot of a staircase with the bird clamped to his crotch 'like a giant nappy'. Its unyielding jaws were eventually prised loose with a screwdriver, but not before they had done considerable damage to 'that which a man values above all else'. 'The moral of the story would seem to be: never tell a goose it has no letters,' quipped the emasculated mailman.

It's not often that birds kill humans, but when they do, they do it spectacularly. Witness events in Heidelberg, Germany, where a man dressed as a giant budgerigar was killed by a swan whilst crossing a bridge in a thunderstorm. Werner Strauss was on his way home from a trade fair where he had been promoting a brand of birdseed when the accident happened. 'It had started to rain heavily,' recalled Mr Strauss's companion, who was disguised as a fan-tailed bird of paradise. 'We were exhausted after a day of cheeping and flapping our wings, and Werner suddenly cried, "God, I hate being a fucking bird!" Then there was a loud squawk and it fell on him.' 'It' was a large white swan which had suffered a heart attack after being hit by a freak bolt of lightning whilst flying overhead. The unfortunate creature landed directly on top of Mr Strauss, causing him to lose his balance and plummet 70 feet over the side of the bridge. 'I knew something terrible had happened as soon as the police asked if my husband was a large household bird with papier-mâché orange feet,' said the man's weeping wife.

Never underestimate pet-shop owners. They might seem like decent enough people, always ready to advise on cat litter and hamster snacks, but beneath that jovial exterior lurks something altogether more sinister. Witness German shop-owner Egbert Schwein, 63, who, in a bizarre re-run of Monty Python's dead parrot sketch, attempted to sell a client a deceased gerbil. Customer Oskar Stoll had spotted that the gerbil was dead almost as soon as he had paid for it. Mr Schwein, however, insisted that the creature was only sleeping because 'it had eaten too many sunflower seeds'. 'It was ridiculous,' said Mr Stoll. 'The thing was lying on its back stiff as a broom handle. I've never seen anything look less alive in the whole of my life.' When he asked for his money back and a replacement gerbil, however, Schwein went berserk, kicking him in the knee and throwing six angel fish at him before following him home on his moped and daubing 'He kills gerbils' in six-foot-high letters across the front of his house. 'I never touched the bloody thing,' said a distraught Mr Stoll. 'It was clearly dead as a dodo before I even got in the shop.'

One of the most dramatic courtroom battles in recent years occurred in Krefeld, Germany, where a long-haired dachshund called Cindy stood accused of eating a neighbour's parrot. According to the prosecution, the attack was the latest in a series of punitive, pet-based expeditions launched by the Volker family against their neighbours the Arsebuns. Hostilities apparently began when the Arsebuns accused the Volkers of training their gerbils to creep under the fence and defecate in their garden. 'There were droppings on the patio and we knew just where they came from,' exclaimed Mr Arsebun, who retaliated by teaching his parrot to scream, 'Up yours, Volker!' in the middle of the night. It was at this point, claimed the prosecution, that the Volkers, 'consumed with hatred for the parrot and all it stood for', dispatched Cindy to gobble up the offending creature. After a nerve-racking two-week trial, however, Cindy's defence counsel was able to demonstrate that her muzzle was in fact far too big to get through the bars of the parrot's cage; and then, in a dramatic denouement, proved that the unfortunate bird had in fact been devoured by Mrs Arsebun in an attempt to frame the Volkers' dog. 'It was like a Hollywood courtroom drama,' said Mr Volker, 'and Cindy was Michelle Pfeiffer.'

As if they didn't already have enough human hoaxers to deal with, the emergency services have now started getting joke calls from dogs. One of the most dramatic of these occurred in Japan, where four fire engines, seven ambulances and 72 policemen sped to a block of flats in Tokyo at the request of a long-haired dachshund named Maurice. Maurice, aged four, had been playing with his owner's phone when he somehow contrived to dial the number of the emergency services. 'There was a terrible wheezing sound at the other end of the line,' recalled the emergency operator. 'Initially I thought it was an asthmatic having a heart attack, but when he growled, "Gas!" I immediately realised the seriousness of the situation.' Believing they were dealing with some sort of massive chemical leak, police immediately rushed to the scene, cordoning off the entire area and evacuating 500 people before breaking into the flat from where the call had originated. 'I was sitting on the loo,' explained the dog's bewildered owner, 'when 20 men in rubber suits burst in and put an oxygen mask on my face. Maurice is very naughty, and won't be having any treats.'

As if it wasn't enough that they do it on lampposts, dogs have now started urinating on rifles, with disastrous results. Witness events in Poland, where a dog shot its owner after the latter castigated it for weeing on his favourite hunting gun. Jacob Wajda, 33, had leant his rifle against a tree whilst inspecting hoof prints in a forest near Radom. On hearing 'a whoosh of warm water', he had turned round to see his dog, Jiri, relieving itself down the gun. 'I shouted, "Naughty! Naughty!"' explained Mr Wajda. 'I must have startled him, because he leapt in the air, banging the gun, which fell over and went off, shooting me in the leg.' Bleeding profusely and unable to walk, Mr Wajda, accompanied all the while by the faithful Jiri, dragged himself to his jeep and was driving at full speed to the local hospital when, by a horrible twist of fate, he came across another dog weeing in the middle of the road. He duly swerved to avoid the creature and crashed headlong into a tree, breaking five ribs and severely concussing himself. He has now given up hunting, because 'God clearly wills it.'

Nasty, vicious, bad-breathed things that they are, Yorkshire terriers certainly don't deserve the fate of Hackney hound Mr Perkins, who suffered a particularly traumatic experience whilst out for walkies with his owner, Ethel Stoat. According to eyewitnesses, 80-year-old Mrs Stoat – who was wearing a tartan mackintosh and furry, zip-up-the-front boots – was heard to cry, 'Slow down, Mr Perkins!' whereupon she tripped over a paving slab and fell face forward on to her dog, killing it with her forehead. The tragedy was compounded when, as she clambered to her feet, the traumatised octogenarian was approached by a local butcher, who indicated the squashed dog and asked, 'How much for the meat jelly?' 'She was very upset, poor old thing,' said a passer-by. 'She kept saying, "I've squashed Mr Perkins! Give me a port and lemon!" '

Normally the most peace-loving and amenable of creatures, pigs, like many of us, can cause a great deal of trouble when they get sexually aroused. Witness 100-pound American porker Charlton, who caused havoc in Miami when he broke out of his pen and forced his attentions on a shiny black Harley-Davidson motorbike. The vehicle in question belonged to short-tempered Hell's Angel Bertram 'Hot Thing' Tonks, 32, who had parked it outside a local bar whilst he went drinking with friends. 'When I came out I saw what looked like a very ugly man in a pink jumpsuit straddling my bike,' explained the inebriated Angel. 'I don't like people touching my wheels, so I attacked him.' From here things escalated rapidly, with a group of passers-by coming to Charlton's defence, convinced he was a beautiful woman being assaulted by a hippie,' and Mr Tonks's drinking buddies hitting the passers-by with baseball bats. In all 14 people were hospitalised, the only combatant emerging completely unscathed being Charlton himself. 'It's them corn husks what makes him randy,' explained his owner.

Feed them kitchen slops by all means, and corn husks and acorns. Feed them a sumptuous eight-course meal served on antique Delft china. Feed them anything you want, but never, ever give a pig marijuana. Brazilian pig-farmer Paulo Sergio Goulart did, with disastrous consequences. Mr Goulart had discovered 40 large bricks of the narcotic wrapped in plastic bags and hidden in his barn. Thinking they were a type of alfalfa, he fed them to his porkers, who immediately began to act in a 'very saucy manner'. 'They ate my wellingtons,' said a terrified Mr Goulart, 'and had sex with my tractor.' The stoned swine then charged *en masse* into the local village, where they destroyed a fruit stall, uprooted several gardens and attacked a priest who ran at them with a crucifix crying 'Jesus is the Lion of Judah!' They eventually fell asleep in the local church and were transported home in wheelbarrows. 'They were overcome by the spirit of the sixties,' explained Mr Goulart.

Some animals are easy to kidnap. Cats, dogs, rabbits, hamsters – just scoop them up and carry them away. Others are less easy, but still possible – horses, for instance, or sheep. Some, however, are absolutely impossible, in which group one would have to include pygmy hippopotamuses, a fact demonstrated all too clearly to American desperado Luther Bee when he tried to abduct one from his next-door neighbour. Mr Bee, 32, of Sacramento formed his dastardly scheme after neighbour Gladys Cain told him her hippo Nebuchadnezzar was 'my very lifeblood'. Choosing an afternoon when Mrs Cain was absent, Bee duly waylaid the corpulent creature and secreted it in his bedroom, demanding a $100,000 ransom for its return. Things began to go wrong almost immediately, however. 'It did massive turds on the bed,' said a disgusted Mr Bee. 'The duvet was ruined. Then it started roaring. We had to tell all the neighbours my wife had tonsillitis.' Over the next 24 hours, Nebuchadnezzar ate Mrs Bee's jewellery, charged the bedroom door down six times and repeatedly tried to mate with his captor, who eventually phoned the authorities and confessed everything. 'He thought it was all a big game,' said Nebuchadnezzar's adoring owner.

They might be the inspiration for Winnie-the-Pooh, Yogi and a host of other cuddly anthropomorphisms, but when it comes down to it bears can be a damned nuisance. Such was certainly the opinion of Mr Markku Tahvainen of Finland, who drove 500 miles to see some bears in a Helsinki zoo, only to be told they had diarrhoea and wouldn't be coming out that day. Mr Tahvainen, 43, had always wanted to see some real bears ever since his grandmother had read him stories about them as a child. After two years of saving, he duly set off to fulfil his life's ambition in Helsinki, only to be told, on arrival, that the zoo's bear population were having bowel difficulties and weren't on show. Not to be deterred, he booked into a guest house and remained in the capital for almost a month, visiting the zoo every day, but all to no avail. 'I saw canaries and geese and exotic insects, but not a single bear,' said the disappointed tourist. 'I thought I spotted one in the penguin enclosure, but it turned out to be a keeper in a fur coat.' Eventually Mr Tahvainen admitted defeat and returned home, where neighbours excitedly informed him that whilst he'd been away his house had been ransacked – by five wild bears. 'They pooed on my pillows,' said the devastated home-owner. 'It was the final insult.'

When dealing with elephants there are certain health and safety guidelines it is always wise to follow: never make them angry; never stand in front of them when they're charging; never approach them with a large currant bun strapped to your forehead; and above all never, ever intervene whilst they're making love. Unfortunately Belgian zoo keeper Maurice Verstpoomer failed to adhere to the last of these rules, getting himself involved in a raunchy three-in-a-pen pachyderm love session with inevitably tragic consequences. Mr Verstpoomer, 41, a born-again Christian and keen computer games player, was cleaning out the elephant enclosure in a Brussels wildlife park when its inhabitants began 'huffing and puffing and doing it with their trunks'. According to eyewitnesses the outraged attendant shouted, 'Not on a Sunday you don't!' before running at the elephants with his broom and endeavouring to discourage their coital activities. 'He got between them and was shouting, "Turn to Jesus!"' said one onlooker. 'But then they mounted each other and he got squashed in between them.' The crumpled keeper was rushed to hospital, but was pronounced dead on arrival. 'He was a good Christian man, killed by mating elephants,' said a terse zoo press release.

The gap between zoos and takeaway restaurants appears to be narrowing, as demonstrated by goings-on in Tel Aviv, Israel, where two zoo keepers have been arrested for eating virtually all the animals entrusted to their care. It appears that Moshe Arun, 36, and Sergei Abramovitz, 43, had tired of the hummus and pitta bread sandwiches their wives gave them each day for lunch and therefore decided to 'check out the small mammal house for something a bit more tasty'. Their initial foray resulted in a 'lovely gerbil goulash with carrots and potatoes', cooked on a primus stove in their office, and was followed the next day by 'a sumptuous armadillo in almonds, chick peas and Madeira'. From there things spiralled out of control as the carnivorous keepers cut an ever-increasing swathe through the zoo's population. 'We couldn't stop,' said Mr Abramovitz.

'One day we ate 40 canaries and five parrots in butter sauce, which were nice, but not as filling as the miniature Persian goats.' They were eventually caught trying to smuggle a wombat out of the zoo 'for a weekend snack' and arrested. 'We didn't eat the hippos,' said Mr Arun in mitigation of his crimes. 'They were just too big to get in the oven.'

Fruit and Veg

Although its regular consumption is supposed to be good for you, fruit can also be extremely dangerous, as discovered by a New Zealand man when he was murdered by a giant organic pumpkin. It appears that farmer Jerry Kulpin, 54, was strolling along a road in Christchurch when a van laden with pumpkins whizzed past him and crashed into a wall. Under the force of the collision a rogue 280-pound fruit tumbled off the back of the lorry and rushed down the street towards the unsuspecting pedestrian, hitting him head-on and killing him instantly. 'I shouted, "Watch out for the pumpkin!" ' recalled one eyewitness, 'but he just laughed and said, "Bugger pumpkins!" and then it squashed him.'

Everyone who's anyone has, at some point or other, been given a parking ticket. Not many people, however, have been issued with a ticket for an illegally parked watermelon, one of the very few being Danish motorist Lotte Bummerbus. Mrs Bummerbus, 71, of Odense, Denmark, had returned to her Volvo after completing the week's shopping and was in the process of loading her groceries into the boot when the offending melon spilled from its paper bag and rolled into the empty parking space behind her. 'I decided to leave it until I had finished loading all my things into the car,' explained Mrs Bummerbus, 'but then I saw the warden giving it a ticket. I said, "Hang on a minute!" but he screamed, "No, you hang on, old witch!" and gave it a £30 fine. Despite a series of complaints to the local authorities, the fine was upheld, with judges ruling that 'illegal parking is illegal parking, whether it be by car, bicycle or melon'.

Sitting stacked up at the grocer's, or on top of poles at the fairground, coconuts seem such placid, hairy things. If used in the wrong way, however, they can be absolutely lethal, as discovered by Malaysian farmer Mat Hussin Sulaiman, who was recently killed by one. Trouble started when Mr Sulaiman, 76, dispatched his pet monkey, Diana, up a coconut palm to pick the nuts. This she did for half an hour, before being joined by a wild monkey, with whom she proceeded to mate amongst the fronds. 'Father banged on the side of the tree,' recalled Mr Sulaiman's son, 'and shouted, "Wicked thing! Pick nuts, not fuck!" But Diana took no notice.' Infuriated, Mr Sulaiman began throwing bananas at the pair, eventually hitting Diana upon the head, whereupon she propelled a coconut at him, shattering his skull. 'It was funny,' said Sulaiman Junior, 'because last year she broke his arm with a lemon.'

In their ongoing and wholly admirable fight against crime and its perpetrators, the police have, on occasion, been known to over-react. Such was certainly the case in Illinois, USA, where local SWAT teams besieged a bus for seven hours in their efforts to capture a man who had stolen a small bunch of seedless South African grapes. Trouble started when the man, described as 'male, plump, Caucasian, with fat, wet lips', snatched the grapes from a display at the front of a greengrocer's and ran into a local bus station. By the time police had arrived, the bus on which it was thought the thief had embarked had already left, whereupon, believing the man to be a dangerous criminal, roadblocks were set up, the bus brought to a halt, armed officers deployed and 'the Godless grape-stealer' ordered to give himself up. When he singularly failed to do so, specialist negotiators were brought in to try to persuade him to surrender, but to no avail. Eventually, convinced he was a 'total psycho', police stormed the vehicle, only to discover that their suspect wasn't on it in the first place. 'Six passengers had grapes,' explained the local sheriff, 'but none of them were seedless and they all had receipts. Still, better to be safe than sorry.'

Vegetables have, to date, played but a small role in the demolition business. Their capacity for architectural destruction, however, was demonstrated to great effect in the town of Salina Cruz, Mexico, where an entire bank was destroyed by a single aubergine. The renegade vegetable, concealed within a small wickerwork basket, had been accidentally left by its owner in a corner of the bank. Convinced it was a bomb, staff immediately evacuated the building and called the police, who, after an initial examination, referred the matter to a crack army bomb disposal unit. The latter arrived amid much mayhem and flashing blue lights, and immediately decided that the aubergine was 'far too complex' to defuse and would have to be made safe in a controlled explosion. Unfortunately, the explosion wasn't quite as controlled as they would have liked and destroyed not only the aubergine but most of the building around it. 'Thank God it wasn't a pumpkin,' said one bystander, 'or they might have blown up the whole town.'

Turnip contests are, on the whole, placid occasions. There are exceptions, however, one of the most dramatic being the Helsinki National Turnip Competition, where Gustave, the winning vegetable, was viciously mutilated by a jealous rival. Trouble started when Gustave's owner, Mr Max Schilstrom, told fellow competitor Yuther Harlberg that his lovingly cultivated turnip looked like Imelda Marcos. Outraged, Harlberg retorted by questioning Gustave's pedigree, claiming it resembled 'a radish on steroids' and should be drug-tested. The two men came to blows and Harlberg was forcibly ejected from the exhibition hall, only to return an hour later carrying a shotgun with which he blasted the unfortunate Gustave to pulpy pieces. 'I feel like I've lost my own son,' said a distraught Mr Schilstrom. 'We had such wonderful times together.'

Anybody who gets into *The Guiness Book of Records* deserves respect, but few deserve it as much as one Mr Parthasarthy, of New Delhi, India, who recently entered the hallowed halls of record-breakers by devouring two giant rose bushes, whole and without condiments. The rose-bush repast marked the culmination of a three-year quest for records by Mr Parthasarthy which had seen him push a mustard seed 500 metres with his nose, swallow 625 chillies in one sitting and break wind continuously for almost two minutes. 'Since I was a child I have wanted to break records,' he explained. 'When I was four I pushed an entire Thermos flask up my nose, and I have followed my dream ever since.' With the rose bushes he finally achieved his goal of a *Book of Records* entry, eating them over a period of some 16 hours, watched by a large crowd of cheering onlookers. 'The pricks will certainly sting on their natural release,' he admitted, 'but I have brought honour upon my family and the State of India.'

As if we didn't already have enough to deal with, what with murderers, rapists, burglars, muggers, terrorists and incurable viruses, a new horror has of late begun stalking humankind – large prickly thorn bushes with pretty flowers on top. Witness events in America, where innocent suburban housewife Carmen Creamey spent an entire weekend in the cruel clutches of a monster rose bush. Mrs Creamey, 40, of Sacramento was weeding in her back garden when she inadvertently trod in a large pile of dog's mess. 'I was scraping it off my foot with a trowel when I lost balance and fell in the bush,' she explained. 'My husband is very particular about his roses and would have gone berserk if I'd damaged any blooms, so I just stayed perfectly still and called for help.' This, however, singularly failed to materialise, and it was only two days later when her spouse, Parker, returned from a fishing trip in the hills that the unfortunate woman was finally rescued. 'He rushed into the garden and screamed, "Oh, my God, are you all right?" ' recalled a sore Mrs Creamey. 'I said "Yes, darling, I'm fine," but then I realised he was talking to the bush. Parker does love his roses.'

The only place where you regularly find food worse than that served by British Rail is in hospital, the Health Service being renowned for the overwhelming disgustingness of its culinary offerings. Fortunately, however, things haven't got quite as bad as they are in Russia, where food at one Moscow hospital was deemed so abominable that patients spent mealtimes foraging in a local forest rather than eat the victuals provided. 'It was disgusting beyond description,' complained 68-year-old angina patient Gvorny Szada. 'The chef had terrible eczema and dandruff and a permanent cold. He sneezed on the food and pushed his fingers in it. One woman found toenails in her soup. Not just one toenail – lots of them, all piled up at the bottom.' At first patients asked relatives to bring in extra food, but when this proved insufficient for their needs, they began sneaking into nearby woods and munching fir cones, bark and wild mushrooms. 'I developed a taste for moss,' recalled Mr Szada, 'and for bluebells when I could get them. Once I found a daffodil and I was in heaven.' Russian health officials have made no comment on the matter, save to award the aforementioned chef a gold medal for his 'remarkably moist suet dumplings'.

Probably the most disastrous botanical expedition of recent years took place in New Zealand, where flower experts Lionel Pucker and Tim Batty finally located a rare species of orchid for which they had been jointly searching for 15 years. Following a tip-off from a fellow botanist, Pucker and Batty had launched a $25,000 expedition to a remote and inaccessible corner of

New Zealand's South Island. Here they had established a camp from which each morning they sallied forth in search of the elusive flower. 'Our aim was not just to locate the orchid,' they explained, 'but to preserve it for posterity. It could well have been the last of its kind, so our expedition took on an almost spiritual importance.' Six weeks of extensive scrutiny, however, failed to turn up any sign whatsoever of the orchid, and eventually they decided to strike camp and call it a day. 'We were lifting up our groundsheet when we spotted what looked like a squashed pair of lips,' said Batty. 'I said, "Bollocks, it's the orchid!" Then we both started crying.' The crushed plant was, apparently, on Pucker's side of the tent and 'didn't stand a chance 'cos he's fat and rolls around in his sleep'.

Work

Job interviews can be traumatic things, although few people can have had as upsetting an experience as did Glaswegian Timothy Cummings. Mr Cummings, 26, had been unemployed for almost nine months when his girlfriend arranged him an interview at a local printer's. 'I was so excited,' said the impassioned interviewee. 'I thought, "At last I can make something of my life. Things are looking up." ' On arrival for his interview, however, Mr Cummings was surprised to be shown straight into a lavatory cubicle, where he was given a 72-page questionnaire to fill out. 'They were impossible questions,' he recalled. 'Things like, "When was Gloria Hunniford born?" and, "Give the postcodes of all of those who died in the *Titanic* disaster." I couldn't answer any of them.' After two hours he was shown into an office, where a panel of three men looked at his responses and pronounced him an 'ignorant shitbag' before making him strip naked for an immediate medical, and then stand in a corner whilst they considered his application. Only when another nude man came in and asked if anyone wanted a cup of tea did he twig that the whole thing was a joke, organised, it transpired, by his girlfriend and her cousin, who owned the company. 'It was OK, though,' said a cheery Mr Cummings, 'because I got the job.' 'Nice arse,' remarked his new employer.

In these days of world recession some people will go to any lengths to keep hold of their job. Few, however, can match the dedication of Italian Claudio Ferro, who for 20 years persuaded fellow office workers he was blind. Mr Ferro, 41, of Rovigo began his pretence in 1975, when he applied for a job as a switchboard operator. 'I thought they'd be more sympathetic if I was blind,' he explained, 'so I went to the interview with a white stick and dark glasses. They were extremely kind, especially when I pretended to fall down the stairs on my way out.' The ruse evidently worked, for Mr Ferro landed the job, thereafter spending the next two decades bumping into doors, knocking things off tables and accidentally rubbing up against attractive women. 'It was wonderful,' he enthused. 'People got my shopping for me and took me on holidays and I always got a huge Christmas bonus. If I'd been in a wheelchair as well I could have retired by now.' His subterfuge was eventually discovered when fellow workers spotted his photo in a paper after he won a national cross-country roller-skating competition. 'We used to find him stumbling around the ladies' lavatory,' recalled one disgusted secretary, 'but we thought, "Poor man, he can't see the door signs." '

Secretary alert! Across the globe typists have been completely losing the plot, as evidenced by Austrian PA Gunthwilde Pummstock, who ran amok when mild-mannered boss Rolf Maister politely asked her to correct a spelling error. Although Ms Pummstock, 53, of Radstad had worked for Mr Maister for 32 years, he had never, in all that time, once asked her to correct something. 'I wasn't nasty or rude,' he recalled. 'I just said, very calmly, "Could you change this please, Gunthwilde?" at which she screamed, "I'm not a fucking gherkin!" and hit me over the head with her typewriter.' As Mr Maister lay dazed and bleeding on the floor, the psychotic secretary proceeded to remove his socks and feed them through the office paper shredder before forcing a large yucca plant down the toilet and throwing her word processor out of the window, where it landed on Mr Maister's new red Porsche. Amazingly, he allowed her to keep her job. 'Deep down she's a honey bee,' he smiled, 'and nobody makes better cocoa.'

From the outside it all looks glitter and swanky banquets and mounds of Ferrero Rocher, but the glamorous world of diplomacy can also be a tough one. It certainly has been for Zaïre's diplomats, as demonstrated by Emany Likambe, Zaïrean ambassador to Poland, who spent three months sleeping rough in a Warsaw railway station. Ambassador Likambe was ejected from his official residence after it was repossessed due to non-payment of rent. 'How could I pay the rent,' he inquired, 'when I hadn't been paid for three years?' He initially set up home in a defunct embassy limousine, bedding down on the back seat and sallying forth each morning on official business. When the car roof started to leak, however, he took to travelling the country on overnight trains, sleeping in the toilet cubicle. 'It was rather inconvenient,' he explained, 'because I had to carry all my official papers, several items of ceremonial equipment and a set of *Encyclopaedia Britannica*s with me. I soon got used to it, though.' When he missed an important meeting because he was asleep 400 miles away, however, Mr Likambe decided to terminate his itinerant lifestyle, duly returning to Warsaw station and settling into a giant tractor tyre with 'Visa Inquiries to Embassy' painted on the side. 'It's quite nice,' commented the ambassador, 'except the porters won't clean my shoes, which makes me very angry.'

These days you just can't get the staff. Or rather you can get the staff, but they don't do what they're supposed to. Such was certainly the case in Bristol, where the town's exclusive Marriot Hotel was forced to sack a newly employed cleaner for being too clean. Mr X (name withheld for legal reasons) had arrived for his first day at work and been asked to clean a lift, a task which took him four days. When asked by his supervisor why this relatively simple job had taken so long, he gamely replied, 'Well, there are 12 of them, one on each floor, and sometimes some of them aren't there.' It seems he had been under the impression that each floor had a separate lift, and had cleaned the same one 12 times. 'We've got the cleanest elevator in the northern hemisphere,' admitted one hotel official.

Just how uncaring some employers can be was discovered by Ohio housewife Alison Holt, who received a telegram from her husband's boss announcing that her beloved Brad had 'blown his stupid block off with a shotgun' whilst at work. Not content with that, the communiqué went on to describe the precise sound Brad's cranium had made as it spattered against the office wall, before demanding compensation for 'the mess his pathetically small brain left on the carpet'. 'I was in shock,' explained the traumatised widow, 'and then I lost control and attacked the fridge with a baseball bat. He was everything to me.' When she had sufficiently recovered her composure, a still-tearful Mrs Holt was driven to the town morgue to identify her spouse's headless body. On arrival, however, she was shocked when the bloodstained cadaver sat up in its drawer, presented her with a bouquet of flowers and announced, 'Who loves ya, baby?' before singing the chorus of Whitney Houston's 'I Will Always Love You'. The whole thing was, it transpired, a joke to celebrate her 30th birthday. 'He's like that,' said a beaming Mrs Holt. 'Last year he spent two weeks pretending he'd been paralysed in a car accident.'

The way forward in employer/worker relations could well lie with Japanese property developer Hotei Kano, 61, who has dramatically improved his company's productivity with the introduction of a series of carefully graded punishments for staff who fail to hit their sales targets. Minor offenders are forced to spend their lunch breaks barking like dogs, whilst successful salesmen pelt them with doggy snacks. Lavatory breaks are permitted, but only if performed 'in a true canine manner'. More serious ineptitude means a day spent on all fours, snorting and informing passers-by, 'I'm a little pink pig, oink-oink.' The most draconian level of punishment, however, is reserved for staff who consistently fail to perform their duties properly, these being forced to work stark naked whilst hee-hawing and wearing a pair of donkey's ears taped to their heads. 'Perhaps it is a little harsh,' admits Kano, 'but it works. Look at me. I'm a millionaire.'

An equally imaginative means of increasing productivity has been developed by Japanese editor Itsuo Sakawa, who has doubled the circulation of his Osaka newspaper by caning his journalists. Desperate both to increase sales of his paper and to improve its editorial quality, Mr Sakawa recently plastered his office with notices declaring, 'Bad stories mean sore bottoms!' Writers who consistently produce boring copy are now publicly thrashed with a large metal ruler called 'Mr Spank', the number of strokes dictated by the tedium level of their journalism. One unfortunate financial writer has received six such beatings, including one eight-stroke session for a snooze-making piece on increment-based insurance policies in Outer Mongolia. 'It's actually very good for morale,' admitted one staff writer. 'You work so much harder when you know your arse is on the line.'

All journalists have, at one point or another, employed a little artistic licence to spice up a story. Few, however, are punished as cruelly for their invention as was Iranian Khedev Orgun, banned from journalism for life for fabricating a story about a talking pillow. Mr Orgun, 40, of Tabriz, Iran, was working on a small local paper when he had the idea for the pillow story. 'I was tired of writing about goat contests and bouncy babies and how so and so had won a government aubergine contract,' he explained, 'so I invented the cushion.' According to Mr Orgun's dramatic article, a local boy had taught one of his mother's pillows to sing. 'It has gold brocade and a strong voice,' said the piece, 'and when it sings of love your heart will melt.' Unfortunately, the article came under official scrutiny after hundreds of readers complained they no longer felt comfortable sitting on cushions if they thought they could speak. Mr Orgun was subjected to an official investigation and, after admitting his fraud, banned for life. 'I've nothing against singing cushions *per se*,' said Mr Orgun's editor, 'but they must be based in fact.'

Where once they went on expensive lunches and naughty weekends to country house hotels, business managers are now eschewing sex and fine wine in favour of physically demanding outdoor assertiveness courses. Weekends of competitive executive game-playing are, it appears, the very best way of strengthening morale, teamwork and mental agility, although the psychological side-effects on losers can be horrific. Such was certainly the experience of American accountant Nathan Lillypad, who topped a humiliating week of executive sports by getting his penis stuck in a swimming-pool air filter. Mr Lillypad of California had proved singularly inept at every aspect of the assertiveness training course on which he had been sent by his company. 'I couldn't do the hand-to-hand combat because I get asthma,' he explained. 'My tent caught fire and everyone called me Miss Piggy.' The final night was spent in a hotel, where a midnight swim went disastrously wrong after Mr Lillypad's penis was inadvertently sucked into the pool's filter as he trod water at the deep end. He was eventually freed, in front of 300 cheering guests, by frogmen using Vaseline. 'It's ruined my life,' moaned the aching accountant. 'I used to be respected but now people make slurping noises whenever I go past.'

We've all come across rude bank staff in our time – the ones who growl when you can't remember your account number and stare blankly at you when you try to engage them in pithy conversation. Rarely, however, has there been a bank employee quite as dreadful as Chinese cashier Ms Weng Foo Bung, who called her customers 'pig testicles' before killing one of them with a small potted cactus. Ms Foo Bung, 25, of Guangxi province in southern China had apparently taken exception when an elderly customer tried to exchange some dirty banknotes for crisp, clean, new ones. 'She poked him on the cheek and cried, "It's not the notes but your pants that are dirty, old pig!"' recalled one eyewitness. 'She looked like a madwoman.' Outraged clients crowded around Ms Foo Bung and began chanting, 'She's the woman with the dirty notes!' at the tops of their voices, whereupon she launched a stream of 'genital invective' before striking one man on the shoulder with her cactus, causing him to suffer a fatal heart attack. 'Whatever the provocation, one shouldn't kill customers,' opined a leader in the local newspaper.

Basil Fawlty was not alone. For some hoteliers, violence is an integral part of the service they offer. Witness Ernesto Galli, 56-year-old proprietor of the Sun Coast Hotel in Sardinia, who dispatched the following midseason memo to staff: 'Residents are eating too many prawns at the cold buffet. They must devour the eggs and asparagus instead. When you see a resident approaching the prawns, whisper quietly, "No, no, they are rotten – the eggs and asparagus are much nicer." If they continue towards the prawns, slap their hands with a spoon and shout "Please!" If that fails, push them to the floor and say, firmly but politely, "No prawns for you!" ' Who says customer service is a dying art?

Usually they're cheery middle-aged men with red faces, soft hearts and a fine line in cockney banter. The traditional image of the Great British milkman was shattered for ever, however, by the antics of dairy deliverer Wilf Sneddon, who burnt down the houses of customers who failed to order enough Gold Top. Trouble started when Carlisle pensioner Nora Jones decided to change her regular order from three bottles of full-cream milk to one of semi-skimmed. 'He became very threatening,' explained a trembling Mrs Jones, 'and told me to rethink or there'd be trouble. I said I couldn't drink that much milk, but he hammered on the wall and said I'd just have to try. Then he set light to my Skoda.' It was the first in a series of milk-orientated attacks by Sneddon, who blew up another customer's lorry for being in arrears with his orange-juice payments and set light to a couple's house after they cancelled their standing order for whipped cream. He was eventually arrested after police caught him battering down a door with a sledgehammer and crying, 'Cheddar cheese is best!' and is now in prison. 'Dairy products are vital for good health,' explained an unrepentant Mr Sneddon.

In a profession renowned for neither its gregariousness nor breadth of imagination, one lawyer stands head, shoulders and buttocks above the rest. The man in question is Peruvian advocate Hernando Rojas, who, in a novel attempt to attract more clients, has produced a brochure featuring himself in various 'tasteful' erotic poses. The pornographic prospectus is the culmination of a series of novel marketing ploys by Mr Rojas which have also seen him disguise himself as a large elephant 'to signify the full weight of the law' and offer free trips to prostitutes for clients whose cases he lost, the latter backfiring badly when customers deliberately started engaging him on unwinnable lawsuits. 'I'd even hired a plane to trail a banner with my name on it across the sky,' said the barmy barrister, 'but unfortunately it crashed into an electrical pylon and the pilot was killed.' The erotic brochure is, however, by his own admission, Mr Rojas's masterpiece. Ten pages long, in full glossy colour, it provides a detailed explanation of the legal services offered by its designer, interspersed with photos of himself in sundry nude poses. 'There's one in my office,' he explained, 'one in the courtroom and one on my motorbike. In all of them, however, I am wearing highly buffed black shoes and holding legal documents. It is important for customers to know that I am a qualified professional.'

Sport

Few things can be more exciting than all-girl soccer tournaments, and few all-girl soccer tournaments can be more exciting than that held in Foggia, Italy, where a 42-year-old man tried to pass himself off as a nubile 16-year-old female goalkeeper. The impostor in question was trainer Piero Pucci, who was forced to don a wig, bra and pair of small, ripe watermelons when his official keeper failed to turn up for an important knock-out match. 'We'd been training for this match for two years and I wasn't going to see us lose because we didn't have a goalkeeper,' explained Mr Pucci, 'so I put on my melons and went out to great applause. I felt like Pelé.' According to the referee, Pucci's short, fat hairy legs were 'not that unusual for a buxom country girl who had grown up in the hills, tending sheep', and the bewigged trainer played the entire first half without any trouble, even managing to save a penalty. Things started to unravel in the second half, however, when Mr Pucci punched one of the opposing team and ordered her, in a deep growl, to 'Back off, bitch.' It was, however, only when one of his melons exploded after a particularly athletic save that Pucci's true identity was revealed. 'It was a shame,' confessed the referee, 'because I found her rather attractive, in a homely sort of way.'

It's not often that you see a football referee blowing his top, but when they do blow, boy, do they blow. Witness German referee Bayram Kaymakci, who shot a player who refused to be sent off in a charity match at which he was officiating. Mr Kaymakci, 28, of Hanover had shown the red card to striker Osbert Vorwerk after the latter had perpetrated a particularly violent foul. When Vorwerk called Kaymakci a 'jelly prick', however, and steadfastly refused to leave the pitch, the incensed referee produced a revolver from his shorts and shot the malefactor in the head. 'One has to maintain discipline on the field,' explained Mr Kaymakci, 'otherwise the game doesn't flow properly and children can't enjoy it.' Fortunately, he only grazed Vorwerk's ear and, after being wrestled to the ground by the victim's team-mates, was banned for three months and fined. 'People criticise me,' he complained, 'but many in the crowd said it was the best match they had ever seen.'

Bruises certainly, and occasionally the odd pulled muscle, but rarely do competitors in a tug-of-war have their hands ripped off, as happened to the unfortunate Stanley Harris. Mr Harris, 21, of Chattanooga, Tennessee, was one of 20 men involved in the competition. 'We were dressed as fluffy sheep,' he explained, 'and the opposition were moorhens. It's sort of traditional.' According to eyewitnesses, each side was tugging as hard as it could when Mr Harris, resplendent in a large white fleece with cardboard horns, suddenly shouted, 'My hand's come off!' 'We all laughed,' said one woman, 'and shouted things like, "That's not very handy!" or, "Want a hand to screw it back on?" But then we saw it hanging on the rope, like a dead crab. It was horrible.' Mr Harris was rushed to hospital, where his hand was surgically reattached in a four-hour operation. 'It must run in the family,' he later mused, 'because my cousin had her nose sucked off by a vacuum cleaner.'

They might not have the best football team in the world, or ever have been in serious contention for the cricket world cup, but when it comes to one sport the people of Finland are quite without rival – woman-carrying. This traditional pastime is now the subject of a World Woman-Carrying Championship, held every year in the lakeland village of Sonkajarvi in northern Finland, where competitors endeavour to lug their women across a 275-yard obstacle course, tackling water-jumps, tunnels, fire-hoops and 'a big thing with spikes on top'. Victor for the past three years – winning 44 bottles of lemonade, a loaf of rye bread and a sauna towel – has been Ilpo Ronkko, 34, whose technique has been described as combining 'ox-like strength, the grace of a gazelle and a selection of extremely small women'. Indeed, so small have Mr Ronkko's riders been that fellow competitors have suggested they were not proper women at all, but rather pygmies in knitted frocks, hence giving him an unfair weight advantage. Mr Ronkko, however, has furiously denied the accusation. 'My women were perfectly legal,' he said. 'I won my lemonade fair and square.'

Normally the most sedate of games, golf can occasionally turn explosive, as demonstrated by events in Zimbabwe, where 49-year-old Eugenius Wimple put three people in hospital after crashing his golf buggy into a makeshift bamboo toilet. It appears that Mr Wimple of Harare had become uncontrollably excited after scoring his first ever hole in one. Having thrown his clubs in the air, removed his trousers and done a victory dance on the green, a euphoric Mr Wimple leapt into his golf buggy and began careering around the course, screaming, 'I done a hole in one, Mum!' to bewildered fellow golfers. 'He didn't see the toilet because it was hidden behind a hummock,' explained an eyewitness. 'He just flew over the hump, screamed, "Christ, a bog!" and crashed straight into it. It was like something out of James Bond.' Four people were using the toilet at the time, two of whom were seriously injured. 'One minute I was on the loo reading Greg Norman's autobiography,' said one victim, 'and then suddenly there was a golf buggy on top of me. Next time I'll go in the bushes.'

For holidaymakers the sea can be a dangerous place, what with sharks and jellyfish and pollution and strong currents. At the Italian resort of

Ravenna, however, these perils paled into insignificance alongside lifeguard Lorenzo Trippi, who was recently sacked for accidentally killing three people with lifebelts. Mr Trippi, a former discus-thrower, had been employed by Ravenna municipal council on account of his 'excellent physique and willingness to do good'. Things started to go wrong from the word go, however. 'Whenever he heard a cry he would rush into the sea,' explained a fellow lifeguard, 'and scream, "Be brave, swimmer in distress, you shall not sink!" And then he'd throw the life preserver at them.' Unfortunately, Mr Trippi, unable to shake off the habits of his discus-throwing days, would launch his lifebelts with just a little too much force and accuracy, each time hitting his target square on the forehead and knocking them out, whereupon they drowned. On several occasions he also threw lifebelts at people who were merely waving to relatives. 'I was signalling my wife to get me an ice-cream with nuts,' recalled one holidaymaker, 'and the next thing I knew a lifebelt hit me in the face and broke my jaw.' Mr Trippi has accepted his dismissal with good grace. 'My mother was ox-wrestling champion of Padua,' he said by way of explanation.

Beautiful baby contests are usually amongst the least violent of competitive events. Such was certainly not the case, however, at the Ploughman's Baby Festival in Canning, Utah, where mother Lisa Samuelson ran amok after someone called her son Chester 'a dirty cushion'. Trouble started when short-sighted judge Ernie Budden inadvertently sat down on Chester, believing him to be 'one of those special medical pillows for people who've had an operation'. On hearing her son's squeals, Mrs Samuelson went justifiably berserk, belabouring the apologetic judge with her handbag, before picking up three babies, one after the other, and throwing them at the event organiser, who fortunately caught them and hid them safely underneath his table. She was eventually restrained by other mothers and arrested, although not before she had set light to a set of curtains, prompting a swift evacuation of the show hall. 'Chester's a well-fed child,' she admitted, 'but he's certainly not a medicated cushion.'

Few bodily phenomena can be more humiliating than malodorous feet. For those taking part in the World's Smelliest Footwear Competition, however, smelliness is next to godliness. Billed as 'A Gargantuan Stinkfest of Unhygienic Shoes', the competition takes place each year in Vermont, USA, and attracts dozens of competitors from around the globe, all submitting their loathsome footwear in the hope of collecting $100 and the title 'Footstink of the Year'. A panel of expert judges carefully sniff the entries, both on the feet and off, awarding points for rancidness, range of odour and overall repellence factor. 'Essentially what we're looking for is an item of footwear so nauseating we can't even get near it,' beamed one judge. 'Champion shoes should be able to make grown men weep.' Current title-holder is eight-year-old Michael Moore, who beat off stiff competition from a pair of Russian workman's boots and some French farmer's sabots. His trainers are now on display in the Vermont Hall of Fumes, where, according to one admiring curator, 'They are the most disgustingly smelly exhibit we've ever had. Like sewage mixed with cheese and dead shellfish.'

Jaywalking – the practice of crossing a road when you're not supposed to – has been responsible for more than its fair share of traffic accidents and deaths. Whilst governments worldwide have implemented schemes to deal with the problem, however, few have come up with anything as imaginative as that employed in Indonesia, where persistent jaywalkers are required to do on-the-spot press-ups as punishment for their crimes. One of the many people who have fallen foul of this draconian measure is 52-year-old Mr Kango Luba of Jakarta, who was subjected to a rigorous regime of physical exertion after accidentally spilling some of his chocolate buttons on to the side of the road. Mr Luba had been perambulating along the street eating his sweets when two of them slipped from his hands on to the road. Barely had he stepped off the kerb to recover them, however, before two policemen charged at him screaming, 'Burpees! Burpees!' There followed, according to Mr Luba, 20 minutes of pure hell as he was publicly exercised before a large crowd of cheering onlookers. 'I was doing squat-thrusts and God knows what,' he recalled. 'People were shouting, "Make the pig run a marathon!" I only wanted my chocolate buttons.' 'Jaywalkers are like drug dealers,' opined one police official. 'They must sweat for their crimes.'

Crime and Punishment

Aside from bungee-jumping with Pamela Anderson, one of the most common of all public fantasies must be to find thousands of unclaimed banknotes blowing down the street. In Australia, however, fantasy became reality when a masked raider dropped a sackful of cash outside a Sydney building society after a bungled robbery. Passers-by gleefully helped themselves to the drifting notes, but were suddenly brought up short by six-foot-four bodybuilder and obsessive law-abider Nathan Mulch, 33, who bellowed, 'Wait, dickos, that cash ain't yours!' As pedestrians stood by shamefacedly, Mr Mulch then gathered the spilled money, put it back into its sack and set off in pursuit of the fleeing bank robber with a cry of, 'Stop, man in a mask, I want to talk to you!' After a dramatic two-mile chase, he eventually cornered his quarry in a high-rise car park, where, much to the robber's surprise, he handed back the money and told him to take more care of his savings in the future. 'I thought he had a mask because he was deformed,' explained the embarrassed hero.

Whatever problems Britain might be suffering on the education front, they are as nothing compared to those currently being experienced in Bangladesh. Understaffed and underfunded we might be, but we have yet to witness scenes such as those in Dhaka, where students sitting a mathematics exam rioted after being told they weren't allowed to cheat. Some 200 students were doing the exam, described by one examiner as being 'so unbelievably easy that even an innumerate warthog with glasses could have passed'. Not so, however, 20-year-old scholar Sanjiit Karim, who stood up mid-exam and asked permission to go to the library to look up some answers. When the adjudicator told Mr Karim 'not to be stupid, it's a bloody exam', he and 100 fellow students went berserk, bombarding the cowering supervisor with rulers, calculators and protractors before barricading themselves at the back of the room and eating their exam papers as an act of defiance. Police were called and in the ensuing mêlée two students were killed and 30 injured. Order was eventually restored and, once the digested exam papers had been replaced, it was decided that candidates could henceforth cheat, provided they didn't leave the examination hall to do it and apologised afterwards. 'How else are we supposed to pass?' inquired one bewildered scholar.

Drinking scrumpy, holding illicit midnight feasts and slapping each other's bottoms in the showers is one thing, but now public schoolboys have started being really naughty. A prime example of this decline in standards can be found in South Africa, where the head boy of an exclusive Johannesburg school kidnapped his history master and made him limbo-dance at gunpoint. Jedediah Roth, 17, was by all accounts a model scholar. 'He was excellent at maths and home economy, and so polite,' explained his headmaster. 'We all thought he had a bright future.' There was thus considerable surprise when, during a school coach outing, Roth pulled a gun from his leather satchel and instructed the driver to take him to Soweto, where he needed to 'finish a major cocaine deal'. His business completed, he then ordered 18-stone history master Magnus Proop, who was in charge of the outing, to limbo-dance underneath the bus, shooting at him all the while and shouting, 'Be more bendy.' He was eventually overpowered by fellow students and expelled. 'And to think he won a medal for his clean shoes,' mused a stiff Mr Proop.

The international smuggler is becoming ever more ingenious in his efforts to carry illegal goods from one country to another. Even the most well-conceived operations, however, can sometimes go wrong, as discovered by ace-smuggler Abdul Dhouti when he tried to pass through Cairo airport with a contraband gold ingot clenched between his buttocks. Customs officers first became suspicious when they spotted Mr Dhouti, on a flight from Jordan, limping through the 'Nothing to Declare' aisle clasping his bottom with both hands. 'We pulled him over,' explained one official, 'and said, "Why are you holding your bottom like that? Has it come unscrewed?" which we thought was quite funny. He said he'd eaten some prawns which had disagreed with him and needed a toilet or he'd make a nasty mess, so we let him go.' Mr Dhouti stumbled a further 20 paces, but was then heard to cry, 'Oh no!' very loudly, following which a £68,000 gold bar popped out of the bottom of his trousers. 'There's obviously something very special about Jordanian Airlines' prawns if they produce stools like that,' observed one policeman wryly.

Possibly the most audacious piece of smuggling of all time occurred in Quito, Ecuador, where a woman tried to carry her husband through customs disguised as a large cuddly toy. Officials were suspicious of Imelda Branques from the first. 'She had a huge suitcase,' explained one inspector, 'and looked extremely furtive.' The suitcase was X-rayed, but revealed nothing untoward other than a 'large fluffy koala bear'. A more detailed inspection, however, revealed a quite different story. 'We opened the case and found a midget with a false black nose and adhesive furry ears,' explained one customs officer. 'It squeaked and said, "I'm Chippy the talking teddy!" but we said, "No, you're not, you're a dwarf." Then he tried to run away.' Mrs Branques and her diminutive husband are now awaiting trial. 'Teddies don't smell of alcohol,' said one po-faced customs officer.

Just when you thought criminals couldn't get any more depraved, up pops the New York porridge burglar. This grotesque individual has been implicated in some two dozen break-ins throughout the city, on each occasion holding terrified householders at gunpoint and forcing them to make him a large pot of porridge, which he then eats before making good his escape without stealing anything. 'We were sitting in our living room watching *The Guns of Navarone*,' explained 71-year-old victim Ethan Pirrip, 'when the doorbell rang. When I opened it a man with a gun burst in and forced me and my wife, Emily, into the kitchen. Then he handed me a box of porridge and told me to make a big plate, with lots of cream and sugar.' The terrified couple complied with their tormentor's wishes, standing trembling in a corner as he devoured the porridge, burped, wiped his mouth and then left. 'He didn't take anything, although he did say the porridge wasn't nearly creamy enough, which made us fear for our lives,' recalled the traumatised householder. Police have warned the public to be on their guard. 'God knows what he might do next,' said one overworked officer. 'Toast, grapefruit, muffins – he's a man who'll stop at nothing.'

The PLO, the IRA, Islamic Jihad, Black September – organisations responsible for some of the worst terrorist outrages of modern times. Rarely, however, did their members sink as low as Guatemalan extremist Pedro Pompoza, who recently robbed a bank armed with a single free-range egg. Mr Pompoza, 32, had burst into the bank in San José and brandished his egg at terrified staff, claiming it was 'a lethal explosive device capable of killing millions of people' and demanding they hand over all their money. 'The egg had wires on it and looked extremely dangerous,' explained the bank manager. 'I thought it might be some sort of nuclear device, so I complied with all his demands.' As staff emptied the bank vault Mr Pompoza did a folk-dance and sang revolutionary songs before collecting his loot and making his way out. As he passed through the front door, however, he unwisely turned around, held his bomb-hand aloft and shouted 'Revolution!' whereupon the egg burst and spattered all over his face and neck. 'We shouted, "What! Eggs!"' recalled one customer, 'and then attacked him with wastepaper baskets.' An unrepentant Mr Pompoza is now serving a 10-year jail sentence.

One of the most important things to remember if you ever find yourself holding up a bank at gunpoint is to make sure you've got a gun to point. Unfortunately, French criminal Oscar César failed to adhere to this simple rule, with disastrous consequences. Mr César, 30, of Marseilles had been planning the robbery for several months, staking out the bank, familiarising himself with its security systems, painstakingly planning his escape route and even arranging someone to launder all the money he intended to steal. On the appointed day he awoke early, went through his plans once more, synchronised his watch and then burst into the bank with a bloodcurdling cry of 'Get your hands on your heads and your heads between your legs or I'll blow your brains out!' Only then did he realise the one flaw in his otherwise masterful scheme – he didn't have a gun. Initially he tried to brazen it out, claiming it was a special invisible gun developed by the Israeli secret service, but when staff showed signs of not believing him he cried, 'OK, OK, wait here, I'll be back in half an hour.' He duly rushed out of the bank, drove home and, true to his word, returned 30 minutes later with a large shotgun. Unfortunately, staff had by this point alerted police and, when he charged back into the bank, a shocked Mr César found himself confronted by 20 armed officers who wrestled him to the floor and arrested him. 'You can't trust anyone these days,' he moaned.

One of the most determined and ultimately unsuccessful of all bank robbers was deaf German Klaus Schmidt, currently behind bars after being arrested because he couldn't hear the burglar alarm going off. Courageously refusing to allow his disability to get in the way of his criminal activities, Mr Schmidt, 41, had burst into a Berlin bank armed with a World War Two pistol and screamed, 'Hand over the money or I'll shoot.' Terrified staff had asked if he needed a bag, to which Mr Schmidt confidently replied, 'You're damn right it's a real gun!' 'We knew then that he was deaf as a doorpost,' explained the bank manager, 'so we set off the alarm. It was unbelievably loud, but he didn't seem to notice, even when some people put their hands over their ears.' The hard-of-hearing robber waited patiently for five minutes, occasionally waving his gun in the air and crying, 'I'm a trained killer!' until eventually police burst in and arrested him. He is now suing the bank for 'exploiting my disability'.

It might sound like fun, but robbing an off-licence can often have disastrous results, as discovered by American thief Crimbert Snozzle, whose efforts to hold up a local liquor store culminated in him being violently sick all over his trousers. Mr Snozzle, 36, a part-time building labourer, had burst into the shop in Kirksville, Missouri, wielding a baseball bat and screaming, 'I'm thirsty, you mothers! Give me a drink!' Barely had he made his request, however, before cucumber-cool shopkeeper Andrew Fadden produced a shotgun and said calmly, 'You want a drink, son, you have a drink.' He then prodded Snozzle into the storeroom, where he made him swill 20 bottles of strong German lager, two of whisky and one each of peach schnapps and Warnink's Advocaat, as well as eating five jumbo packs of buttered popcorn. 'It was the popcorn that did it,' explained a gratified Mr Fadden. 'He went very green, said, "Please, sir, can I stop now?" and then puked all down himself like a big baby.' 'I've learned my lesson,' said a chastened Snozzle. 'Now I want to work with underprivileged children.'

Being a thief doesn't mean you can't be nice as well. Witness robber Adolf Slubbert, who, by abandoning a robbery in order to drive a heart-attack victim to hospital, displayed the sort of public-spirited generosity often markedly absent from the behaviour of normal, law-abiding citizens. Mr Slubbert, 32, of Sydney had burst into 71-year-old pensioner Bertram Muth's home wielding a machete and screaming, 'Move and you're spare ribs, Grandad!' Barely had he announced himself, however, before Mr Muth clutched his chest and fell to the floor, groaning, 'Oh, my poor heart!' Without a second thought, the benevolent burglar discarded his weapon, cried, 'Be calm, old man, I shall save you,' and rushed the pale-faced septuagenarian to hospital on the back of his motorbike. Unfortunately, however, his generosity came to nought for, on reaching their destination, Mr Muth hopped lithely off the back of the bike, cried, 'Fooled you, sucker!' and summoned hospital orderlies to arrest his horrified rescuer. 'That sort of thing really dents your confidence,' admitted a disillusioned Mr Slubbert.

The image of the hitman as a cucumber-cool purveyor of swift and violent death was shattered for ever by the antics of Australian assassin Boris Sleazby, probably the worst professional killer in the world. Mr Sleazby, 41, had been hired by a wealthy Sydney industrialist to murder his business partner. From the word go, however, it all went horribly wrong. Initial plans to run the man over were shelved when Sleazby's wife wouldn't lend him her Nissan

Cherry, whilst attempts to shoot him with an air rifle came to nought because each time he fired at his target 'the pellets just bounced off his head like marbles'. A knife attack failed when Sleazby fell down a manhole; an elaborate scheme involving a high-tech letter bomb was stymied by a wildcat postal strike; and a dramatic attempt to drown his victim ended with the hopeless hitman being stung by a jellyfish and helped from the water by the man he was trying to kill. Eventually Sleazby's millionaire employer lost patience with his assassin, calling him 'about as dangerous as a fucking dropsied teddy bear' and sacking him, whereupon an outraged Sleazby went berserk and killed the man with a single karate chop. 'I guess it was poetic justice,' he later commented.

Probably the most disastrous ever attempt to steal petrol from a car was made by Antipodean hard-man William Goose. Mr Goose, 26, of Auckland, New Zealand, had broken into a local campsite late one night with the intention of siphoning off petrol from the cars of sleeping campers. Fumbling around in the pitch darkness, he discovered what he took to be the cap of a car's petrol tank, unscrewing it with a snigger, inserting his hose and sucking forcefully to get the gasoline flowing. Unfortunately, what he had actually located was not a petrol tank at all but a portable sewage-holding facility. 'We heard a cry of, "Oh, Christ, it smells disgusting!"' recalled camper Alice Fairbairn, 'and then someone being sick on the concrete.' Taking a flashlight, she went out to investigate, discovering Goose 'curled up like a woodlouse' in a pool of his own vomit and pleading, 'Please help me, I think I've eaten shit.' He was immediately rushed to hospital, where his stomach was pumped by amused hospital staff. 'We aren't pressing charges,' said the campsite owner. 'He seems to have suffered enough already.'

Possibly the worst day in the history of organised – or rather disorganised – crime was experienced by Miami thief Natron Fubble, 35, surely a prime candidate for the title of 'World's Most Inept Robber'. The day started with an early morning raid on a delicatessen which was cut short after the shop-owner hit Mr Fubble in the face with a giant salami, breaking his nose. An attempted bank robbery ended before it had even begun when he met his mother in the same bank and was sent to do some shopping for her, whilst a mugging went horribly wrong when he slipped in some dog's mess and concussed himself against some railings. The climax, however, came late in the afternoon when, pursued by irate customers after another failed hold-up, he took refuge in the boot of an empty car. Unbeknown to the clueless criminal, however, the car was in fact a police surveillance vehicle whose owners, returning from a cup of coffee, drove for five days across America tailing a suspicious lorry. His whimpers were eventually heard just south of Seattle, where he was removed at gunpoint and arrested. He was forthwith sentenced to two years in prison, despite claiming he was on a top-secret undercover mission for the FBI.

Despite the fact that they're breaking the law, it's good to know that some criminals still observe the basic rules of decency and politeness. Witness American bank raider Alvin Toffeebee, 43, who behaved quite impeccably whilst holding up the Central Bank of Montgomery, Alabama. Having entered the building, Mr Toffeebee waited patiently in a queue until it was his turn to be served, at which point he took out a gun and told the cashier to hand over her money or he'd blow her head off. She politely told him he was in the wrong queue and needed one at the other end of the bank, for which Mr Toffeebee thanked her and joined the correct line, waiting for a further 20 minutes until police burst in and arrested him. 'He just couldn't understand how we got there before he'd even done the robbery,' commented one officer. 'What a total bozo!'

The only thing more degrading than being robbed is being told you're not good enough to be robbed. Such was the humiliating experience of Nigerian father of 12 Kango Ube, who was informed that he couldn't be burgled until he purchased something worth burgling. Mr Ube, 35, of Lagos was sleeping in his front room when two men armed with machetes burst in and demanded money. Their terrified victim explained that he was unemployed and penniless, whereupon the intruders called him 'shit on a shoe' and subjected him to a gruelling two-hour lecture on the importance of self-respect. 'I offered them my duvet,' recalled Mr Ube, 'but they said they would rather sleep in dung with an old woman and told me to get a job so I could buy nice things for them to steal.' Amazingly, he took the thieves at their word, finding work as a cleaner and purchasing a variety of expensive household items, so that 'next time they will show respect and think my possessions a great prize'.

Forget screeching burglar alarms, Neighbourhood Watch schemes and bruising self-defence classes, the best way to foil thieves is to eat the things they want to steal. Such was the novel and highly effective course chosen by Spaniard Miguel Angel, who foiled a group of muggers by devouring his entire wage packet before they could lay their hands on it. Mr Angel, 27, of Irun was walking home from work when he was confronted by the robbers in a gloomy subway. 'There were three of them,' explained Mr Angel, 'real nasty types with flick-knives. They said, "Give us your money, wanker!" but I replied, "Bugger that!" and swallowed it. It was tasty.' To his assailants' amazement, he then proceeded to eat his watch, necklace and two gold rings before offering to mail them his possessions 'once they'd come out the other end', at which point they ran away. 'They called me a loony,' said a satisfied Mr Angel, 'but at least I'm a loony who's never been robbed.'

Some people will go to quite extraordinary lengths to protect their property. Twenty-foot-high electric fences, razor wire, infra-red video cameras – they're all available for the security-minded householder. Even the most paranoid of property owners, however, would think twice about surrounding their home with landmines, as did Bulgarian turnip-farmer Gazna Poorga, with disastrous results. Forty-two-year-old Mr Poorga of Kavarna had filled his vegetable fields with high-tech Russian personnel mines as a deterrent to flocks of ravenous crows. 'I bought them on the black market and planted about 100 of them,' he explained. 'A bird only had to land close to them and they'd go off with a huge bang. It was funny to watch the crows exploding.' Unfortunately, however, he failed to inform best friend, Lukner Silas, about the mines and was thus horrified when, following a night's heavy vodka-drinking, the latter rushed into the field with a cry of, 'Let's run free among the turnips!' 'I shouted, "Stand still and don't move!"' recalled a tearful Mr Poorga, 'but he just cried, "Be free, Gazna!" and then he blew up.' The force of the blast destroyed Mr Poorga's farmhouse and rendered him unconscious. 'Next time I'll use scarecrows, with big straw hands and buttons for their eyes,' said the flattened farmer.

One of the most spectacular and innovative jail-breakers of all time has to be American midget Quentin Bender. Mr Bender, 35, who stands just over three feet tall in his stockinged feet, has spent most of the last 15 years in and out of prison for a succession of offences ranging from armed robbery to kidnapping an old lady's guinea pig and holding it for ransom. Bars, walls and armed guards have presented no obstacle to the determined dwarf, however, and his novel bids for freedom have now attained the status of legend. On one memorable occasion he endeavoured to escape through the prison sewer system wearing a home-made aqualung, and on another disguised himself as a large racoon in the hope that kind-hearted warders would release him back into the wild. All had ended in failure, however, until he hit upon the butter scheme. For three months Bender hoarded a variety of miniature butter and margarine sachets before eventually smothering himself in their contents and slipping to freedom through the food-hatch of his cell. He has so far eluded capture. 'We've warned the public to be on the look-out for a nude, butter-covered midget,' said his determined prison governor, 'but we're not hopeful. He's a cunning little devil.'

Probably the only prison escapee who could compete with Mr Bender in the innovation stakes is US murderer John Woodcock, 32, until recently an inmate of Charleston Penitentiary, Virginia. Officers at Mr Woodcock's prison had been baffled by a spate of thefts of dental floss from the infirmary. 'It was very curious,' said the prison doctor. 'We were losing up to 100 boxes of floss a week. Someone, somewhere, must have had extremely clean teeth.' An investigation was launched, with suspicion immediately falling upon Matthew Snope, a mild-mannered accountant who worked in the infirmary whilst serving a three-month sentence for motoring offences. Despite protesting his innocence, the latter was put in solitary confinement and had all his privileges withdrawn.

The real culprit was revealed two days later, however, when Woodcock made an audacious escape using a rope ladder spun from the pilfered dental floss. His first act on gaining his freedom was to send a postcard to the prison governor: 'Sorry, dick-brain, but I done the floss. Snope's clean. Thanks for the ladder. Up yours, Woodcock.' He remains at large.

Escaping from prison is one thing, but staying escaped requires an inordinate amount of imagination and skill. Witness convict-on-the-run Gustank Babbage, who endeavoured to outwit his pursuers by hiding in his girlfriend's fridge with his head stuck up a large turkey. Mr Babbage was halfway through a seven-year sentence for armed robbery when he broke out of the high-security penitentiary in New Mexico. He sought refuge in his girlfriend's flat in Albuquerque, where he remained for two weeks until, following a tip-off, the building was raided by police. An extensive search of the woman's flat, however, failed to reveal any sign of the escapee, and it was beginning to look as if he'd given his hunters the slip when, on a whim, police officer Simon Jobbins opened the fridge. 'It was full of watermelons,' he explained, 'dozens of them, with a sort of upside-down turkey on top. I thought it was a bit weird, but couldn't see what it had to do with Babbage and was about to close the door when the turkey started shaking, like it was giggling. Then it sneezed, all the melons came tumbling out and there he was.' It appeared that, having seen the police arriving out of the window, Mr Babbage's girlfriend had pushed her lover into the fridge and concealed him behind a wall of melons, with his head jammed up the bottom of a 20-pound turkey. 'At first he claimed he was just a magician practising a new trick,' said Officer Jobbins, 'but then he admitted who he was and we arrested him.' He is now finishing his sentence in solitary confinement.

It's not often you find criminals actively seeking to get themselves into jail, but that's just what happened with law-abiding burglar Thierry van Schuler, who was repeatedly refused entry at a Brussels prison, despite having been convicted on several charges of breaking and entering. Mr van Schuler wasn't in court when he was sentenced *in absentia* to four years in prison on eight counts of aggravated burglary. On hearing of the verdict, however, he immediately did the decent thing and presented himself at the appointed prison, politely informing warders that he had been convicted of theft and needed to be let in to begin his sentence. To his considerable chagrin, however, he was informed that he didn't have the requisite paperwork and could therefore not be accommodated. 'I said, "Don't be fucking ridiculous," ' recalled an outraged Mr van Schuler. ' "I'm a dangerous criminal. Handcuff me immediately!" But they just said rules were rules and if I didn't have a blue form with pink and yellow duplicates I couldn't come in.' There ensued a bizarre three-day quest in search of the requisite paperwork, with van Schuler informing every policeman he passed, 'I'm dangerous! Lock me up!' and every policeman he passed telling him to go home and sleep it off. He eventually located the necessary permits and succeeded in getting himself incarcerated, but even then the cell wasn't to his liking. 'It's far too good for scum like me,' he declared.

Cock-ups and Capers

Two of the most unlikely – and, as it turned out, innocent – smugglers, were septuagenarian widows Kitty and Beryl Tuber of Kent, who were stopped at French customs after a pilgrimage to Lourdes. Following an anonymous tip-off, customs officers pulled the jittery sisters from their car and emptied the boot, where they discovered a hoard of hard-core pornographic videos, 15 boxes of latex dildoes and an assortment of rubber bondage equipment. According to Beryl, 'I thought at first that Kitty had bought something for our niece's pony, Pumblechook. But then the man waved what looked like a large rubber rolling pin in my face and said, "Husband no good, eh?" I said, "My husband's dead!" and started crying. Then he blew up what looked like a pink beach ball and it was a naked woman with blonde hair. It was then that Kitty fainted.' Fortunately, the two old ladies were released without charge, and plan to go to the Lake District next year. 'They don't have those sort of things in Kendal,' said a shocked Kitty Tuber.

Ever since Orson Welles's legendary forties radio adaptation of *The War of the Worlds*, as a result of which large sections of the US public actually believed there had been an attack from outer space, Americans have been obsessed by the possibility of alien invasion. Few, however, react in the manner of Texan Linus Roote, who shot himself because he thought the Earth had been invaded by giant fish from outer space. Mr Roote, 71, first became suspicious when he spotted several 'enormous mutant salmon' moving down the street outside his house. When these were followed by a car driven by a tuna and a red mullet on a mountain bike, he hurried to the bottom of his garden with a shotgun, screamed, 'You won't get me, space fish!' and shot himself in the stomach. He was rushed to hospital, where, after a three-hour and fortunately life-saving operation, he was informed that the piscatorial extraterrestrials were in fact students on their way to a 'Come as Your Favourite Fish' party. 'I thought they wanted to do sex experiments on me,' explained a convalescing Mr Roote.

Fear of alien abduction was also behind the curious behaviour of Mr Chester Thistle of Wisconsin, who shot his beloved brother Franklin after mistaking him for 'a deep-space jelly'. Franklin, 53, was visiting brother Chester to celebrate the latter's 60th birthday. Accompanied by his wife, sister and three children, he had parked his car on the street and was moving up his sibling's darkened driveway carrying six luminous party jellies when the group suddenly came under heavy shotgun fire. 'I saw what looked like a cluster of miniature UFOs,' explained Chester, 'and I just panicked. I thought, "Christ, they've finally landed!" so I told my wife to phone NASA whilst I laid down some covering fire.' Five of the jellies broke formation and fled, but the sixth was seen to tumble earthwards, where it was later found splattered over the prone body of Franklin, who had received gunshot wounds to his legs. 'Chester ran up and cried, "Did they get you, Franklin?"' explained the recuperating jelly-carrier. 'And I shouted, "I *am* they, you bloody corn cob!"' 'I guess I over-reacted,' admitted the contrite birthday boy, 'but these days you can't be too careful.'

Aside from people who break wind in confined spaces, few things can be more annoying than noisy neighbours. Whilst most of us tend to buckle under and put up with the disturbance, however, some take more direct action. One such was Austrian Gunthwilde Blom, 63, who decided violent measures were needed after three days of uninterrupted heavy-metal music from the flat next door. Initially Ms Blom, of the village of Klagenfurt, hammered on the walls with her Zimmer frame and pushed increasingly vituperative notes beneath the door of the offending flat. When this had no effect, she confronted her neighbour, Wilma Kock, directly, dismissing her protestations of innocence as 'creamed sewage' and branding her 'a venomous herring'. Still the noise continued, however, and eventually Ms Blom lost control, purchasing 20 pounds of fresh herrings and pushing them one by one through her tormentor's letter box whilst the latter was out doing flower-arranging at the local church. Returning to find her hallway knee-deep in fish, a horrified Ms Kock immediately called the police, who, whilst interviewing Ms Blom, discovered that the music was in fact coming from a radio she had inadvertently left on beneath her bed. 'That's beside the point,' argued the paranoid pensioner. 'She's a noisy cow and flushes her toilet all night.'

Most wives, it would appear, love nothing more than to be surprised by their husbands. Unexpected chocolates, flowers out of the blue, unplanned holidays in romantic places – such things are the lifeblood of a good marriage. There are, however, exceptions, as demonstrated by events in Italy, where a married woman got more than she bargained for after advertising for a lover because sex with her own spouse was like 'bouncing up and down on a collapsed soufflé'. Carla Francetti, 37, received a sackful of replies to her advert, but the man who described himself as 'The Bison of Love' sounded by far the most promising and an assignation was duly arranged in a romantic country hotel. 'I knocked on the bedroom door,' explained Mrs Francetti, 'and a very sexy voice growled, "It's open, my turtle dove!" It was dark inside, but then I saw it on the bed and got very excited.' 'It' was a stark-naked man spread-eagled face-down with a pair of false horns strapped to his head and a bottle of chilled champagne wedged between his buttocks. Overcome with passion, Mrs Francetti hurriedly approached, only to discover on closer inspection that 'those weren't just any buttocks' and that the bison of love was in fact her husband, Francesco. 'I was growling huskily,' explained a disappointed Mr Francetti, 'but then she smashed the bottle on my head and said she wanted a divorce.'

Sometimes one has to make sacrifices for one's art, and in this criminals are no different from anyone else. Witness Frenchman Pepé Semblat, 35, who disguised himself as an old lady in order to infiltrate a Parisian rest home and rob its safe. Wedged in an excruciatingly tight corset and constrictive serge stockings, Mr Semblat succeeded in gaining entry to the home, passing a pleasant evening playing whist in the communal lounge before breaking into the office when everyone else had gone to sleep. Unfortunately, however, he was spotted by a nurse, who told him it was 'time for old ladies to be tucked up tight', and put him to bed in the women's dormitory. He tried to leave the next morning, but was stopped by a porter, who gave him some pills, a cup of coffee and a ball of wool, and he remained a prisoner in the home for two days until his true identity was finally discovered when nurses tried to give him a bed bath. 'It smelt of hideous old ladies,' said a rueful Mr Semblat. 'Frankly, I'm happier in prison.'

A similarly unfortunate cross-dressing experience was had by Moroccan criminal Mustapha Pixibelle, whose scheme to steal guns from a local army barracks culminated with him on his knees scrubbing toilets. Mr Pixibelle of Rabat wanted the guns to sell on the black market and had duly conned his way on to the base dressed as a cleaning woman. As he surreptitiously approached the weapons' store, however, he was accosted by two large soldiers who called him 'a wicked, slacking old crone' and told him that the lavatories stank and needed 'a damn good scrubbing out'. 'I mumbled, "My poor hips!" ' said Pixibelle, 'but they said, "Balls to hips!" and took me to the toilets and told me to get cleaning.' This he conscientiously did for the next six hours, watched over all the while by one of the soldiers. 'There were a lot of toilets,' he recalled, 'and so dirty!' When he had eventually polished the last rim, the watching soldier kissed him tenderly on the cheek and called him 'mother' before escorting him off the base. 'Things didn't quite go according to plan,' admitted Mr Pixibelle, 'although it's lucky I didn't disguise myself as a prostitute or I could have been in real trouble.'

From time immemorial humankind has displayed a fascination for mythical creatures. Dragons, yetis, unicorns, Loch Ness monsters – our thirst for the zoologically unknown remains as strong as ever. Few of us, however, could claim to have actually seen one of these legendary beasts, unlike myopic pensioner Stanley Pile of Nebraska, who not only saw a giant dragon but also captured one alive. Mr Pile, 71, first spotted the fabulous creature in a field at the back of his house. 'It was huge, with terrible wings and thick scaly skin,' he said. 'I was scared, but I am an American and knew it was my duty to capture it for science.' The determined pensioner duly purchased a shotgun and a large net, and then hid himself in some bushes and waited patiently for the dragon to return, which it did two nights later. 'It blundered around and made some bellowing noises,' recounted the intrepid hunter, 'so I shot at it and ran over with the net.' Barely had he reached the monstrous reptile, however, before it shouted, 'Christ, don't kill me!' and two local firemen emerged. The latter were, it appeared, practising for a local pageant inside a dragon costume made by children from a local school. 'Fortunately, he missed us by about 400 metres,' chuckled one fireman. 'I shot wide deliberately,' said a defiant Mr Pile.

One of the most disastrous school talks of all time was given by American Lawrence Bilbo, whose lecture on 'Why We Shouldn't be Cruel to Animals' culminated in him being shot in the buttock by a belligerent caretaker. An ardent animal rights campaigner, Mr Bilbo, 36, travelled the length and breadth of America giving talks to schoolchildren on animal welfare. 'I used to dress up as Willy the Warthog,' explained the caring conservationist. 'I had a furry brown costume, and tusks, and little trotters that I wore over my shoes like galoshes. It gave the whole lecture a bit of topicality and the children loved it.' On the day in question, Mr Bilbo had arrived to give a talk at a school in Cruger, Mississippi, secreting himself in the toilet and donning his Willy the Warthog costume before scampering into the corridor with a loud snort, ready to address the school's 200 children. Unfortunately, he was spotted by short-sighted caretaker Albert Miggins, who, convinced he was actually 'a lion or something', fetched his shotgun and pursued a terrified Mr Bilbo into the school playground, where he shot him in the backside. The lacerated lecturer has since discarded his warthog costume in favour of a bright-orange three-piece suit. 'It's safer that way,' he explained.

We've all done embarrassing things whilst drunk, although few of us can have been as spectacularly humiliated as 26-year-old Manchester hod-carrier Desmond Spoon. Wishing to surprise his friends on their return from a holiday in Corfu, 18-stone Mr Spoon had drunk 15 pints of lager and broken into their flat. Here, chuckling to himself all the while, he had stripped naked and positioned himself in the corner of their living room with a lampshade on his head and a sign saying 'Pull to light' taped to his penis. Half an hour later he heard voices in the hall and the living-room door flew open. To his surprise, however, it was not his friends who walked in but three large men dressed as cowboys who, having put on some music, threw themselves on to the sofa and began kissing passionately, quite oblivious to their guest's presence. Mr Spoon remained stock still for five minutes but eventually, desperate for the toilet, muttered, 'Sorry, must have got the wrong flat,' and shuffled towards the door. 'Fortunately, they didn't try to turn me on,' he later quipped.

One of the great delights of being in love with someone is that you can play little lover's jokes on them, the idea being that you both have a good chuckle and then get in the bath together. Things don't always go according to plan, however, as discovered by the Wisconsin Romeo who dressed himself up as a spider and got a nine-inch gearstick stuck up his bottom. Eusebius Thrum had adopted his arachnid disguise in order to frighten fiancée Eunice Givens. 'Eunice hates spiders more than anything in the world,' explained the bow-legged Casanova, 'so I hired a tarantula costume and hid in the garage rafters till she came for her car. Then I shouted, "Ooooh, I smell a lovely fat fly!" and dropped down.' Unfortunately, instead of dropping to the concrete floor as he intended, he landed on his girlfriend's car roof, which gave way under his weight and deposited him, backside-first, on to the gearstick. 'I went hysterical,' recalled Eunice, 'but then the spider said, "I've hurt my butt," which was a great relief.' Mr Thrum had to be cut free by firemen and has fortunately made a full recovery. 'All the nurses thought it was some sort of sex perversion,' said the outraged prankster.

Although they can occasionally get a little grouchy, telecom operators are rarely as mischievous as the Canadian woman who made a customer undress whilst she listened on the phone. Harry Bole, 36, of Toronto had called the operator to complain about continual interference on his line. 'I heard some whispering in the background and then she started sniggering,' he explained, 'but when she told me to take off my clothes because they caused static, she seemed so reasonable I didn't argue.' Once he was stark naked, the operator then instructed Mr Bole to open all the windows of his house, smear margarine on his walls 'as a sound-wave conductant' and bounce vigorously up and down for two minutes 'to test unit reception'. He gamely complied and it was only when he heard several voices chorusing 'Loser!' down the receiver that he realised he was the victim of an elaborate practical joke. 'The funny thing is,' he said, 'my phone's been fine ever since.'

Frankly, a court of law is the last place on earth you'd think of going if you wanted cheering up. Or at least it *was* the last place on earth you'd think of going until Italian lawyer Gino Camolini came on the scene. Mr Camolini, 41, demonstrated just how much fun you can have with the law whilst acting for the defence during an extended murder trial in Florence. Convinced the mood in court was too sombre, Mr Camolini engineered a series of 'ice-breakers' to try and lighten things up a bit. He started out by placing a large rubber whoopee cushion on the judge's seat and, after the latter sat heavily upon it, asking for an adjournment 'to air the chamber'. He then secreted four dead squid in the prosecution's briefcase before cross-examining a key witness in rhyming couplets. His *pièce de résistance*, however, came on the final day of the trial when he attended court dressed in a grass skirt with a bone through his nose and a false wig. The long-suffering judge held him to be in contempt and jailed the bizarre barrister for three days to teach him a lesson. 'Even in murder trials people should have a good laugh,' declared an unrepentant Mr Camolini.

Death

They might not sound very exciting, but cheese-throwing competitions can be full of surprises. Such was certainly the case at the annual contest in Kolo, Poland, where a member of the crowd was tragically crushed by an ill-aimed ball of Gouda. The Kolo cheese-throwing festival, said to date back over 1,000 years and to have been an essential date in the calendar of Poland's medieval kings, is usually an occasion of joy and festivity, with competitors throwing 10-pound cheeses as far as they can whilst wearing traditional costumes made entirely of cheese rind. On the day in question, the contest, one of the closest for years, had reached its climax, with the final competitor needing a throw of over 70 feet to win. 'He launched his cheese into the sky,' said an eyewitness, 'but the direction was wrong and it went towards an old man. We shouted, "Cheese!" but he said, "No, no, I like pickled herring!" and then it hit him.' By a bitter coincidence, the victim was the thrower's father. 'I killed Papa with a big ripe cheese,' said the distraught son.

Some men will go to quite extraordinary lengths to prove how tough and macho they are. They play rugby, they pump weights, they get in fights, they shower in ice-cold water, and some do all four at the same time. Few, however, can match the exploits of Polish farmer Krystof Azninski, who staked a strong claim to being Europe's butchest man by cutting off his own head with a chainsaw. On the day in question, Azninski had been drinking heavily with friends in a farm outhouse when it was decided that they should strip naked and 'play some men's games'. Initially they contented themselves with hitting each other over the head with frozen swedes and jabbing each other's bottoms with a pitchfork. Things took a turn for the worse, however, when one man seized a chainsaw and cut off the end of his foot. Not to be outdone, Azninski grabbed the saw and, with a cry of 'Watch this then, you women!', swung at his own head and chopped it off. 'It's funny,' said one companion, 'because when he was young he put on his sister's underwear, but he died like a man.'

Death by car crash is terrible at the best of times, but it's somehow even more upsetting if you die whilst dressed as a giant spring vegetable. Such was the tragic demise of 17-stone Gianni Rioseco of Naples, who was tragically killed whilst changing into an asparagus costume at 90 mph. Mr Rioseco, 23, a baker by profession, was on his way to a fancy-dress party when the accident happened. According to witnesses in the car behind, Mr Rioseco was driving along the motorway when he started 'squirming around and taking all his clothes off". Having stripped down to his boxer shorts, he then perched on his seat, steadied the steering wheel with his foot and tried to pull his fancy-dress asparagus costume over his head. Unfortunately, however, he got it on the wrong way round and, blinded by thick Lycra sprouts, veered across the central reservation and crashed into a wall. 'When your lover dies dressed as a vegetable it is a bitter blow,' commented the victim's distraught girlfriend, herself disguised as a large beef tomato.

They might look reasonably innocuous with their cheese and tomato toppings and crusty bottoms, but pizzas have a darker side, as demonstrated in Israel recently when a man was kneaded to death inside a giant pizza-dough mixer. The tragedy happened in Jerusalem's Mystic Pizza, where soldier Moshe Dor-On was visiting friend Chaim Levi. 'I was showing him the mixer and he kept saying how tasty the dough smelt,' explained Mr Levi. 'I said, "It is tasty!" which is when he leant in and tried to scoop some out.' Unfortunately, Mr Dor-On's tie got caught in the kneading blades and he was sucked into the apparatus, screaming, 'My uniform's all doughy!' before disappearing into the mixture, never to be seen alive again. 'I loved him like a brother,' wept a distraught Mr Levi, 'but now he is a deep-pan crusty pizza base.'

We all know that motoring can be a hazardous business. If the case of Abner Kriller is anything to go by, however, it is particularly perilous for short-sighted people who chew bubble gum. According to wife Eunice, spectacle-wearing Mr Kriller, 33, of Sydney, Australia, was a gum fanatic. 'He couldn't get enough of it,' she explained. 'Sometimes he'd have as many as five packs-worth in his mouth at the same time. It made his cheeks go all funny, like he was playing a trumpet.' It all seemed like good, harmless, sticky fun, however, until disaster struck early one morning on a precipitous mountain road. Mr Kriller was on his way to compete in the quarter-finals of the New South Wales King of Bubbles Competition. 'It was his big moment,' said a tearful Eunice. 'He saw it as his chance to break into the big time and get into gum professionally.' According to a fellow motorist, Mr Kriller was driving along steadily when a large purple bubble began to emerge from his mouth. 'It just got bigger and bigger,' recalled the man. 'I was watching it in my rear-view mirror and I've never seen anything so big. It was bigger than his head and he had to move it to one side with his hand so he could see the road. That's when it blew up.' The giant bubble, it seems, burst all over its blower's face and glasses, blinding him and causing him to lose control of the car, which veered through a crash barrier and over the edge of a cliff. 'He was my everything,' wailed his distraught widow, 'but now he's gone to the great Hubba-Bubba in the sky.'

Probably the most disastrous ever attempt to decorate a flat occurred in Austria, where DIY fanatic Hans Pender managed to wrap himself to death in an enormous strip of wallpaper. Mr Pender, 41, of Salzburg was decorating the flat of wheelchair-bound octogenarian Gertrude Steiff when disaster struck. 'He was doing the hallway when a fold of wallpaper fell on his head,' explained his employer. 'He said, "Bugger, it's sticky!" and tried to twist round to get it off, but the more he twisted the more wrapped up he got.' Despite Mrs Steiff's frantic efforts to aid him, Mr Pender became increasingly entangled in the paper before collapsing on the floor and suffocating. 'It was a thick, peach-coloured paper with floral inlay,' recalled Mrs Steiff. 'He looked rather nice in it.'

Some criminals will go to extreme lengths to avoid capture, although American shoplifter Roberto Puelo is probably the only one to have killed himself with a spicy frankfurter sausage rather than stand trial for his misdemeanours. Mr Puelo's extraordinary demise occurred at a 7-Eleven convenience store in St Louis, where the 32-year-old thief had been seized by security guards after trying to shovel an eight-pack of lavender toilet tissue down his trousers. Breaking free from his captors, however, a frenzied Mr Puelo had run to the delicatessen counter, seized an enormous frankfurter and, with a cry of 'I ain't doing chokey for no bog roll!', proceeded to force the giant sausage down his throat whilst holding horrified staff at bay with a carving knife. 'It was like a sword-swallower,' explained one eyewitness. 'It just went further and further into his mouth, and he went purpler and purpler in the face. I'll never eat sausage again.' The meat-impaled malefactor eventually collapsed on the floor with just the end of the sausage sticking out of his mouth 'like a dummy'. He was immediately rushed to hospital, but was pronounced dead of asphyxiation on arrival. 'It was an absolutely massive piece of meat,' said one doctor. 'He didn't stand a chance.'

It's a pretty sad comment on the state of a nation's public transport system when a bus driver can die midway through his route and nobody notices. Such was the case in Argentina, where passengers sat patiently in their seats for seven hours after their driver popped his clogs at the wheel. Trouble started when José Peccaro, 51, of Buenos Aires pulled into the side of the road complaining of chest pains. 'He was wheezing and clutching at his collar, and then he suddenly fell forward and went quiet,' described one eyewitness. 'We all thought he was just having a nap, so we talked quietly amongst ourselves and waited for him to wake up and get moving again.' Three hours later they were still waiting, and a small group of impatient commuters got off, only to be replaced by new passengers. One woman did suggest they call a doctor but was roundly dismissed as a 'scaremongering old crone' and pushed off the bus, and it was only when an irate businessman stormed forward and tried to strangle Mr Peccaro that the awful truth emerged. 'It was a strange coincidence,' said one man, 'because last week we had a driver with only two fingers.'

However apparently healthy you might be, never imagine you can get one up on death. Someone who did, with tragic results, was Swede Kurt Jarlsonn, who plunged to oblivion from a seventh-floor flat dressed as the Grim Reaper. Mr Jarlsonn, a truck driver of Stockholm, had dreamt every night for 30 years that he'd die before he was 50. So surprised and overjoyed was he to still be alive on the morning of his 50th birthday that he arranged a massive jamboree to celebrate his continued survival. 'It was eerie,' said one guest. 'Kurt was dressed as death, with a big black hood and a scythe, and was running around shouting, "I'm alive! I'm alive! Touch me, I'm alive."' All went well, however, till the end of the evening's festivities, when, standing on a chair to deliver a speech, a drunken Mr Jarlsonn boastfully cried, 'Death will never take me!' whereupon he lost his balance and tumbled backwards through an open window. The tragedy doesn't end there, however, for as the bellowing birthday boy plunged earthwards, still clutching his scythe, he was spotted by 85-year-old Ingmar Guntersson, who cried, 'Just a few more years!' before suffering a terminal coronary. 'That's one party I won't forget,' said Mr Jarlsonn's best friend, Derek.

Wherever it's done, and by whatever means, you can't get away from the fact that suicide is a tragedy. Some self-slaughters are more tragic than others, however, with perhaps the most tragic of all being that of the German man who killed himself during a party at his local Suicide Survivors' Club. Marcus Spitz, 41, had been a member of the club for two years, ever since failing to kill himself by jumping off a bridge. On the night in question, the club was holding its annual fancy-dress jamboree, to which Mr Spitz went dressed as a robot. 'It wasn't a very good costume,' recalled club organiser Gunther Marx, 'and for some reason I thought he was Julius Caesar. I said, "Et tu, Brute!" which seemed to depress him quite a lot.' Things went from bad to worse when, after queuing for two hours for food, Mr Spitz finally reached the buffet table to discover all that was left was a squashed vol-au-vent and a taramasalata dip in which someone had extinguished their cigarette, whilst when he asked a woman to dance she refused because his breath smelt of garlic. The final straw came when he slipped over in the toilet and broke his jaw, whereupon he rushed back into the party and, with a cry of 'This is the worst night of my life!', seized a carving knife and stabbed himself in the heart. 'Everyone saw the funny side,' admitted a cheerful Mr Marx.

Funerals are, in general, supposed to be sedate and dignified affairs. Such, however, was not the case on Artur Finke's big day, when he was inadvertently left in a morgue whilst a coffin full of prawns was interred in his place. Croatian-born Mr Finke, 75, had died in Bottrop, Germany, but, in accordance with his last wishes, an undertaker had been hired to transport his body back to Croatia for burial in his native village. Everything went according to plan until, 560 miles into the journey, the undertaker discovered he had forgotten to put his client in the coffin. 'I thought about going back,' he explained, 'but I was late already and I didn't want to keep them waiting at the other end, so I decided to improvise.' Improvisation involved pulling into a small town and casting around for something 'body-like' to take the place of the morgue-bound Mr Finke. 'I thought about a tailor's mannequin,' said the undertaker, 'but it wasn't heavy enough, so eventually I settled for three large sacks of shellfish.' The unwitting crustaceans were duly placed in the empty coffin and given a full Christian burial in front of some 200 mourners. The terrible truth emerged only when the undertaker was later caught disposing of the real body back in Germany. 'I wouldn't have minded except that Artur hated fish,' wailed the dead man's sister.

It might look harmless on the supermarket shelf, and positively alluring when covered in pesto sauce and a smattering of freshly grated Parmesan, but there's another side to spaghetti, and it's not always a pleasant one. Such was certainly the experience of Mexican chef Juan Ruiz, who was speared to death by strands of uncooked spaghetti when his restaurant was hit by a freak hurricane. Mr Ruiz, 51, was preparing courgettes in the kitchen of the Humming Mango when the hurricane struck. Whilst everyone else put metal pots on their heads for protection and cowered beneath tables, Mr Ruiz blithely continued dicing vegetables, seemingly oblivious to the 150 mph winds. 'It was mayhem,' described one waiter. 'Spaghetti was flying around like arrows. We shouted, "Watch out for the pasta!" but he just screamed, "Should I be afraid of tortellini?" and then it got him.' Coroners concluded that Mr Ruiz had been killed by five separate strands of spaghetti which had punctured his heart, lung and eye. 'We've taken Bolognese off the menu as a mark of respect,' said his distraught widow.